IMPRINT:
BOOK SHELTER GMBH
AUFHÄUSERSTRASSE 64
30457 HANOVER
GERMANY

THIS BOOK IS FOR

_____

FROM

_____

Contents

Foreword

This book sheds light on the life of our beloved Prophet Muhammad (saw), whose infinite wisdom, goodness, and righteousness still inspire us today.

There are repeated references in the text which, together with the maps - one of the entire Arabian Peninsula (Map 1), one of Mecca and the region (Map 2), and another of Medina (Yathrib) and the associated region (Map 3) - indicate specific locations of Muhammad (saw). The maps can be found on the last pages of this book.

In Islamic tradition, abbreviations are used after the names of certain personalities to show them respect and honor. These abbreviations are shorthand for supplications or honorific titles.

The abbreviations used in this book are explained in more detail in the following list:

Allah (swt)

Transliteration: Subhanahu wa Ta'ala.

Translation: Blessed and exalted be He.

Muhammad (saw)

Transliteration: Sallallahu Alayhi wa Sallam.

Translation: Allah's blessings and peace be upon him.

The faithful companions and wives of the Prophet Muhammad (saw), such as Abu Bakr (ra)

Transliteration: Radiyallahu Anhu.

Translation: Allah be pleased with him.

Other prophets, such as Ibrâhîm (as) or Adam (as)

Transliteration: Alayhis Salam.

Translation: Peace be upon him.

Further explanations of terms can be found in the glossary at the end of this book. We wish you an instructive, entertaining, and inspiring read.

A long, long time ago, in a world very different from the one we live in today, there lived a man who would change history. His name was Muhammad (saw), and he became the last prophet of Allah (swt). The story of Muhammad (saw) is one of wisdom, courage, and infinite kindness. It begins in Mecca, a city in the desert that today belongs to Saudi Arabia. (See 1. on map 1)

In the time before Muhammad (saw) was born, the people of Mecca lived very differently than we do today. They did not know the message of Allah (swt) as it should come to us through Muhammad (saw). Many worshipped false gods and idols instead of believing in Allah (swt), the one true God. People were often unjust to each other and many disputes and injustices occurred in their communities.

But Allah (swt) had a plan to help people find the right path. It started with the birth of a special child, born into a world full of challenges. But he was destined to give hope and guide people. This child was Muhammad (saw); who would touch the hearts of those around him and the hearts of billions of people worldwide. Muhammad (saw) was born into a prestigious family, but he was to experience the hardships of life at an early age. Despite this, or perhaps because of it, he grew up to be known for his honesty, compassion, and deep love of justice. These qualities would be of infinite value to him on his path to becoming the messenger of Allah (swt).

Muhammad (saw) 's story is not just about the past. It is the story of Islam, which still teaches us a lot today. It shows us how important it is to be kind and just, how valuable knowledge is, and that faith in Allah (swt) can accompany us and help us through the most difficult times.

We now embark on the exciting journey through the life of our Prophet Muhammad (saw) and discover how Allah (swt) chose him to deliver His final message to mankind. It is a story full of challenges, adventures, great achievements, and incredible accomplishments that changed the world forever.

Chapter

1

The Birth and Early Childhood of Muhammad (saw)

On a quiet night in the year 570, later known as the Year of the Elephant, something miraculous happened in Mecca. A boy was born whose life, and deeds would shape the history of mankind. His name was Muhammad (saw), and his birth marked the beginning of a new chapter in the history of Islam and humanity as a whole.

Muhammad (saw) was born into a family of the Quraysh, a respected tribe in Mecca. His father's name was Abdullah, who in turn was the son of Abdul-Muttalib. Abdul-Muttalib was not only a distinguished and respected man from the Quraysh tribe but also the guardian of the Ka'ba. In addition, Abdul-Muttalib's family could trace their lineage back to the former prophets Isma'il (as), his father Ibrâhîm (as), Nûh (as), and Adam (as). Abdullah married Amina, the daughter of one of the leaders of the Quraysh tribe. The two were happily in love and soon Amina was pregnant. While she was still pregnant, she suddenly heard a voice telling her to give her child the name Muhammad and to place him under the protection of Allah, the only God.

But even before Muhammad (saw) saw the light of day, his father Abdullah passed away. Amina and Abdul-Muttalib were heartbroken by the loss, but the imminent birth of Muhammad (saw) gave them comfort and new strength.

Then the time had come: Muhammad (saw) saw the light of day on the 12th Rabi' al-Awwal of the Islamic lunar calendar (year 570). His grandfather, whom Amina had previously talked about the voice she had heard during her pregnancy, took little Muhammad (saw) straight to the Ka`ba - he suspected that his grandson was destined for great things.

According to the ancient tradition of his tribe, Muhammad (saw) was sent to the desert when he was still a small baby to grow up with a Bedouin family of the Banu Sa'd tribe. The fresh air and harsh conditions of the desert were considered healthy for body and mind. With his nurse Halima and her family, Muhammad (saw) came to know and appreciate the simple pleasures of rural life. The family was very poor, but they took good care of little Muhammad (saw). And when they took in the baby, something miraculous happened: Halima, whose mother's milk had previously been barely enough to feed her infant, suddenly had more than enough for both. The camel mare and the goats also gave significantly more milk than before the arrival of little Muhammad (saw). Halima realized that her protégé was a very special baby.

Muhammad (saw) learned the importance of hospitality, honesty, and a close connection with nature. These early years shaped his character. One day, as Muhammad (saw) was playing with other children, two angels suddenly appeared in human form. They wore shining white robes. The angels grabbed Muhammad (saw) gently but firmly, laid him on the ground, opened his chest, and removed his heart. They removed a black spot from it, representing sin and inclination to evil, which they described as part of the Shaitan (Satan).

They then washed his heart in a bowl of Zamzam water, a holy water from a spring in Mecca, from which the young Prophet Isma'il (as) had drunk many years earlier.

After the angels had cleansed Muhammad's (saw) heart and put it back into his chest, they closed his body, left him unharmed, and disappeared. The other children who had witnessed this ran to Halima in horror. They told her that Muhammad (saw) had been killed. Shocked by this terrible news, Halima and her husband rushed to the scene. There they found Muhammad (saw) alive and well, albeit pale and somewhat exhausted from the experience he had just had. This spiritual cleansing was part of the preparation for his future role as a prophet of Allah (swt).

However, his foster mother was worried and decided that it would be better to return Muhammad (saw) to his mother Amina earlier than planned. So, she set off for Mecca. When Halima handed Muhammad (saw) over to his mother Amina, she told her about the strange incident. She explained to Amina that her husband and she had interpreted the event as an ominous sign. They feared that something supernatural or even evil was threatening little Muhammad (saw) and that they had therefore decided to return him to Amina - after all, they had taken him into their hearts and were also responsible for the welfare of their foster child.

Amina showed understanding for Halima's worries. She reassured her by expressing her conviction that her son would have a special destiny. Amina told Halima that a voice told her during her pregnancy that her son would one day play an important and unique role. Amina interpreted the events as a sign of her son's special status and the protection Allah (swt) was granting him, and not as something frightening.

When Muhammad (saw) was six years old, his mother took him on a journey. She wanted to visit the grave of her deceased husband Abdullah, who had died on a trading trip in Yathrib and was buried there. (See 2. on map 1)

After Amina and Muhammad (saw) had spent some time in Yathrib, they began their return journey to Mecca. But first, fate had further trials in store for the young Muhammad (saw). On the way back to Mecca, his mother fell seriously ill and died shortly afterward in the village of Abwa, which is about halfway from Yathrib to Mecca. Muhammad (saw) was now completely orphaned, and his heart bore the scars of deep loss. Along with the other travelers, he finally arrived in Mecca. In his sadness, he found comfort and protection with his grandfather Abdul-Muttalib, who lovingly took him in and cared for him.

His grandfather's position enabled Muhammad (saw) to hold a valued and respected position in Mecca society, despite being orphaned young. This was often not possible for orphaned children at that time. But then the young Muhammad (saw) suffered the next blow of fate. Two years after Abdul-Muttalib had taken in his grandson, the old, wise man died. Now his uncle Abu Talib took over the role of Muhammad's (saw) tutor. Abu Talib was the leader of the Banu Hashim clan, a clan of the Quraysh, and loved Muhammad (saw) as his own son. He made sure that he wanted for nothing, even though his family was not particularly wealthy.

Despite these early losses and challenges, Muhammad (saw) grew up to be a strong and compassionate young man. He played with the other children, learned the work of the shepherds, and watched the hustle and bustle of the streets of Mecca. From an early age, he showed a deep interest in the welfare of the people around him and the big questions of life.

These years of childhood and adolescence laid the foundation for the man Muhammad (saw) was to become. They trained him in patience, compassion, and perseverance - qualities of immense value for his future task as a prophet. Allah (swt) prepared Muhammad (saw) in a way no one could have foreseen. But all this preparation was for a special mission that would positively change the world.

Thus begins the extraordinary story of Muhammad (saw), the last prophet of Allah (swt). His early years were characterized by love, loss, and constant learning. All this prepared him for the path Allah (swt) had destined for him.

Chapter
2

The Early Years of Muhammad (saw)

After the heavy losses of his childhood, a new chapter began in the life of Muhammad (saw).

When Muhammad (saw) was 12 years old, he was allowed to join his uncle on a trip to Syria. Abu Talib was an experienced trader and for Muhammad (saw) this trip offered a valuable opportunity to gain an insight into business life and get to know different cultures outside the Arabian Peninsula. It was the first trading trip for the young Muhammad (saw).

When they had already been traveling for several weeks, the caravan passed near Busra, a city in present-day Syria. There, Muhammad (saw) met Bahira, a Christian monk known for his extensive knowledge of the Christian scriptures. (See 3. on map 1)

The monk had been watching the caravan closely, as he had noticed something unusual: one of the travelers seemed to be shaded by a cloud the whole time, while the others rode through the heat of the blazing sun. When the caravan stopped to rest, the monk noticed that a tree under which Muhammad (saw) was resting was bowing down to him. Moreover, this tree was not just any tree - Bahira knew that other prophets had rested under it many years before. He interpreted all this as a clear sign and did not hesitate for long. Bahira approached the caravan and invited all the travelers to a meal. He was keen to learn more about the person who had been supernaturally protected from the scorching sun.

During the meal Bahira had prepared for the entire caravan, the monk took the opportunity to get to know Muhammad (saw). Having already observed the unusual signs such as the shadowy cloud and the strange behavior of the tree, Bahira sought further confirmation of his suspicions about Muhammad's (saw) special role. He asked to see Muhammad's (saw) back, as he wanted to make sure that he was wearing the special feature he suspected was between his shoulders: the seal of prophethood, which in the traditions serves as confirmation of the last prophet of Islam. And indeed! Right between his shoulder blades, Bahira discovered a distinctive birthmark, undoubtedly the mark he had been looking for.

The monk turned to Abu Talib. He told him that he should watch over his nephew well and ensure nothing bad happens to him. Bahira also told Muhammad's (saw) uncle that he was destined for greatness and that not all people might be favorable to the Prophet of Allah (swt) - which made it even more important to protect Muhammad (saw). Abu Talib took the monk's words seriously and cared even better for his beloved nephew.

Muhammad (saw) Meets his First Wife

In the following years, Muhammad (saw) worked for his uncle and led many caravan journeys. These journeys took him on camels through the vast, unforgiving desert to distant trading centers on and off the Arabian Peninsula. There he met people from a wide variety of backgrounds and faiths. These encounters broadened his horizons and taught him about tolerance, patience, and the diversity of human cultures and beliefs. These experiences were valuable for Muhammad (saw). They trained him in communication and negotiation, strengthened his social skills, and encouraged his natural inclination to reflect and think deeply about life and the creation of Allah (saw).

A special moment in Muhammad's (saw) young years was meeting with Khadija (ra), a wealthy and respected businesswoman also from Mecca. Khadija was impressed by Muhammad's (saw) reputation as an honest and reliable caravan leader, and she was looking for someone to entrust with the management of one of her trading caravans to Syria. This was a task that required both skill and integrity.

To test Muhammad's (saw) suitability for this role and to gain his trust, Khadija (ra) decided to take an unusual step. She offered to lead a trade caravan to Syria. In return, Khadija (ra) gave Muhammad (saw) a salary twice as high as she had paid others for this task. In addition, she provided him with her servant named Maysarah, who had the task of observing Muhammad (saw) on the journey and reporting everything about his behavior and business practices to Khadija (ra). Khadija (ra) was a righteous woman, and honesty and sincerity were important to her.

Muhammad (saw), now 25 years old, finally accepted the offer and traveled with the trading caravan to Syria. During the journey, he impressed Maysarah with his skill, fairness, and way of dealing with people. Muhammad (saw)

showed great patience and demonstrated the valuable ability to keep a clear head and make wise decisions even in difficult situations. Maysarah witnessed Muhammad's (saw) exceptional character and deep spirituality, including some special incidents that foreshadowed the special role he was to play. Maysarah made a remarkable observation: despite the intense, unrelenting heat of the desert, it always remained pleasantly cool around Muhammad (saw).

After returning from the journey, Maysarah told Khadija (ra) about what he had seen and experienced. His positive reports about the young caravan leader Muhammad (saw) only reinforced Khadija's (ra) impression of him as a man of exceptional honesty, integrity, and spiritual maturity. This profound trust and admiration she felt for Muhammad (saw) led Khadija (ra) to fall in love with him and propose to him through a friend. Muhammad (saw) did not have to think about it for long and accepted. He had always felt deep respect, admiration, and personal affection for her. Khadija (ra) was known in Meccan society for her wisdom, honesty, and business acumen. A successful and independent businesswoman, the widow was held in high esteem, not least because of her generosity and compassion towards the poor and less fortunate. These qualities made her an exceptional figure in Mecca society at the time. During their marriage, Khadija (ra) and Muhammad (saw) had four sons and two daughters. Unfortunately, their sons died in infancy.

Muhammad (saw) was already known throughout the city for his sincerity. This was a quality that was highly valued in the business world of Mecca. This virtue, coupled with his kind and compassionate nature, made him an esteemed personality. He cared for the poor and needy and was always ready to help wherever he could. Many traditions tell how he and his family often shared their food with the poor. Muhammad (saw) also had a particularly big heart for orphans and widows, as he had experienced losing loved ones. He encouraged his fellow human beings to care for those with family and emphasized the importance of giving them special protection.

Over the years, Muhammad (saw) gained a reputation as an exceptionally honest and trustworthy man. This is why the people of Mecca named him "Al-Amin" - meaning "the trustworthy" - long before the revelations began. His exceptional character traits laid the foundation for people's willingness to believe the message he was later to deliver. During these years in the life of Muhammad (saw), he already had visionary dreams characterized by their clarity and truthfulness. These dreams were another harbinger of his future role as a prophet and helped to prepare his heart and mind for the coming revelation. But some time was still to pass.

When Muhammad (saw) was 35 years old, a heavy rain poured down on Mecca. The floods severely damaged many buildings and the Ka`ba, built many years earlier by the Prophets Ibrâhîm (as) and Isma'il (as).

The Quraysh, who worshipped their idols at the Ka`ba, quickly began the renovation work and were almost able to rebuild it after a few days of hard work. Then it was time to put the sacred black stone back in its place. And that is when a big fight broke out between the different tribes of Mecca! Each tribe wanted the honor of putting the black stone in its place and to be remembered for it forever. The dispute became increasingly heated and almost came to a fight. Then a wise old man got the crowd's attention with a good idea. He suggested that the next man to come to Ka'ba should decide who would be allowed to place the Black Stone in its place. Everyone agreed to this.

Everyone rejoiced when "Al-Amin" appeared at the Ka'ba. In Muhammad (saw) they saw a fair mediator. He listened carefully to the problem and thought for a moment. Then he had a wonderful idea. He laid a large cloth on the ground and placed the Black Stone in the middle. Then he asked a representative of each tribe to hold part of the cloth. Together they lifted the cloth and brought the stone close to the designated place in the Ka'ba. Muhammad (saw) then carefully placed the stone with his hands. In this way, Muhammad (saw) mediated between the tribes and prevented further disputes.

Chapter 3

The First Revelation

Muhammad (saw) often sought solitude in a cave on Mount Hira near Mecca to meditate and reflect on life and faith. One day in the year 610, when he was about 40 years old, he experienced something extraordinary that would change the world forever. (See 1. on map 2)

On a bright, starry, and silent night during Ramadan, the angel Jibril suddenly appeared to him. The angel brought a message from Allah (swt). Jibrīl asked Muhammad (saw): "Read and recite!" (in Arabic: "Iqra'!"). Muhammad (saw), who could neither read nor write, replied confused and worried: "I cannot read."

Then the angel pressed Muhammad (saw) tightly against him, so much so that he could hardly bear it, and then released him with the renewed request: "Read and recite!" Again Muhammad (saw) replied that he could not read. This process was repeated a total of three times. On the third occasion, Jibril presented the first revelations of the Quran, which can be found in Sura 96:1-5 (Al-Alaq - The Blood Clot) and read:

Sura 96:1-5 (translated):
"Read in the name of your Lord, Who created, created man from a clot of blood. Read, and your Lord is the Most

Muhammad (saw) memorized the words immediately. Then Jibril disappeared as quickly as he had appeared.

With this revelation, the prophetic mission of Muhammad (saw) began. But at first, he rushed home to his wife Khadija (ra), somewhat frightened and confused. He felt overwhelmed by this unusual and deeply spiritual experience. His wife, who was always faithful and supportive, listened to him attentively and encouraged him. She firmly believed in his words and reassured him with the conviction that Allah (swt) would never abandon him as he was a sincere man of truth and goodness.

Then Khadija (ra) sought advice from her cousin named Waraka ibn Nawfal, a scholar of the Christian scriptures. After Waraka heard Muhammad's (saw) narration, he confirmed that Muhammad (saw) had been visited by the same angel who had once appeared to the Prophet Mūsā (as) and delivered a message in the name of Allah (swt). Waraka prophesied that Muhammad (saw) would one day become the prophet of his people.

Muhammad (saw) only shared his revelations with his family and close friends in the beginning. The first to believe in him and embrace Islam were his wife Khadija (ra), his cousin Ali ibn Abi Talib (ra), his close friend Abu Bakr (ra), and his adopted son Zaid ibn Haritha. These early followers supported him unconditionally and were the foundation of the new Muslim community. Their acceptance of Islam was a courageous step when the new faith was still completely unknown in Mecca. When Muhammad (saw) publicly preached the teachings of Allah (swt) sometime later, he met with considerable resistance from the Quraysh. Khadija's (ra), Ali's, Abu Bakr's, and Zaid's professions of faith in Islam were therefore no longer just personal acts of faith, but also significant events that confirmed the legitimacy of Muhammad's (saw) revelations and encouraged other people to also turn to Islam and finally renounce idolatry. At first, however, Muhammad (saw) did not preach Islam publicly, but only in small circles. During this time, the early Muslims met secretly to pray and listen to the teachings of Muhammad (saw). The meetings often took place in private homes to avoid attracting attention. One of the most famous places for these secret meetings was the house of al-Arqam ibn Abi al-Arqam, an early convert, found at the foot of Safa Hill in Mecca. (See 2. on map 2)

Then, around 613, three years after the first revelation, Muhammad (saw) received the instruction from Allah (swt) to proclaim His message publicly. This revelation was delivered to him by Jibril and can be found in Sura 15:94 (Al-Hijr - The Rock):

Sura 15:94 (translated):
"So, proclaim openly what you have been commanded,
and turn away from the idolaters."

After this revelation, Muhammad (saw) ascended the hill of Safa, one of the two hills in Mecca, to speak publicly to the people. He called together the various clans and families of the Quraysh and proclaimed the message of

Islam to them. He began his speech with a rhetorical question to gain their attention:

"O Quraysh, if I told you that an army is behind this mountain and wants to attack you, would you believe me?"

The Quraysh answered unanimously with "Yes!" because they knew and appreciated Muhammad (saw) as Al-Amin, the trustworthy one. Thereupon Muhammad (saw) declared:

"I am a warner who warns of a severe punishment. There is no god but Allah, and I am his messenger. Abandon your idols and turn to the one true God."

The reaction to this public proclamation was mixed. Some people, especially those who had heard of Muhammad (saw) before, began to think seriously about his message. Most of the Quraysh, however, especially the leaders and wealthy merchants, reacted with open hostility and rejection. They saw Muhammad's (saw) message as a threat to the existing social and economic order, which was strongly linked to pagan practices and idolatry.

The Quraysh began to persecute and harass the early Muslims, both physically and economically. Many believers were tortured and abused to force them to renounce their new faith. Among the most famous victims of this persecution was Bilal ibn Rabah (ra), a former slave who endured cruel torture for refusing to renounce his faith. Bilal ibn Rabah (ra) was originally from Abyssinia (modern-day Ethiopia) and was a slave. After hearing the teachings of the Prophet Muhammad (saw), he embraced Islam. This was a very courageous step, as he went against the dominant religious order and the wishes of his master. Bilal's steadfast faith and refusal to abandon Islam made him one of the Prophet's most remarkable companions. Umayyah ibn Khalaf, Bilal's master, was one of the fiercest opponents of Islam. When he learned of Bilal's conversion, he decided to punish him severely to force him to deny his new faith and return to pagan practices. The torture that Bilal (ra) suffered was brutal and cruel. Umayyah had Bilal (ra) flogged and beaten to break his will. He then ordered Bilal (ra) to be taken to the scorching desert during the day's hottest hours. There he was laid on the hot sand with heavy stones on his chest to make it difficult for him to breathe. But Bilal (ra) remained steadfast, and he kept repeating the word "Ahad, Ahad" (One, One), expressing his unshakable conviction in Allah (swt) as the only God.

The Prophet Muhammad (saw) and his companions heard about the slave's fate and were deeply moved by Bilal's suffering and steadfastness. They knew that they had to do something to help him, otherwise his master would kill him. Abu Bakr (ra) decided to ransom Bilal (ra). He went to Umayyah ibn Khalaf and offered him a large sum for the slave. Umayyah, who regarded Bilal (ra) as incorrigible and saw no prospect of forcing him to abandon Islam, agreed to the sale. Abu Bakr (ra) immediately granted Bilal (ra) his freedom. This was a significant moment, not only for Bilal but also for the Muslim community. The former slave was to become a close companion of the Prophet Muhammad (saw) and later even the first muezzin of Islam.

The message that Muhammad (saw) had received from Allah (swt) via the angel Jibrīl and now openly proclaimed in Mecca was clear and revolutionary at the same time. It called on people to accept the belief in one God (tawhid) and to turn away from the polytheistic practices that were widespread in Mecca. Islam emphasized justice, compassion, the duty to support the needy, and the pursuit of a righteous life. However, Muhammad's (saw) revelations still drew opposition and persecution from the Meccan upper class, who saw their traditional lifestyle, their idols, and ultimately their power under threat.

Even Muhammad (saw) faced blatant hostility from the Quraysh. One day when he was praying in the Ka`ba, Abu Jahl approached from behind. Abu Jahl was one of the fiercest opponents of Islam and he intended to humiliate

Muhammad (saw) by stepping on his neck while the Prophet was praying. Abu Jahl stole up to Muhammad (saw) while in sujud (prostration in prayer). But suddenly he saw a deep ditch of fire and terrifying figures between him and Muhammad (saw). Frightened, Abu Jahl retreated and protected himself with his hands. When later asked what had happened, he replied: "Between me and him was a ditch of fire and terrible things and wings." Muhammad (saw) later commented on the incident, saying, "If he had come any closer to me, the angels would have torn him apart." Jibril had been protecting Muhammad (saw) and had appeared in a terrifying and intimidating form that frightened Abu Jahl so much that he retreated and fled.

The Quraysh decided to take further steps against the Muslim community in Mecca to isolate them more and more. They decided to impose a boycott on the Muslims to make their lives as difficult as possible. All measures were recorded in a boycott document. In it, the social and economic sanctions against the Prophet Muhammad (saw), his followers, and the Banu Hashim and Banu Muttalib clans were laid down. The leading members of the Quraysh signed the document, which ordered a complete ban on trade with the Banu Hashim and the Muslims and a ban on marriages between the Quraysh, the Banu Hashim, and the Muslims. After the document was drafted and signed by the leading members of the Quraysh, they kept it in the Ka'ba to emphasize its importance.

The boycott against the Prophet Muhammad (saw) and his followers, including the Banu Hashim clan, led to the Muslims and their supporters being forced to emigrate to Shi'b Abi Talib (Abi Talib Valley). (See 3. on map 2) The boycott lasted about three years, from 616 to 619, and posed immense challenges to the Muslim community. The Shi'b Abi Talib valley was a remote and barren valley near Mecca. The Muslims and their supporters retreated there to escape the persecution and economic sanctions of the Quraysh. The conditions in the valley were extremely arduous and demanded a great deal from them. As trade and the sale of food to Muslims was forbidden during the boycott, the people in the valley suffered from extreme hunger. They were often forced to subsist on leaves and other barely nutritious items. The valley's inadequate diet and harsh living conditions led to health problems. Many of the Muslims, especially the elderly, the weak, and children, suffered from malnutrition and disease.

But despite the difficulties and challenges in the valley, the Muslims remained steadfast in their faith. Muhammad (saw) remained confident and encouraged his followers to do the same. He conveyed trust in Allah's (swt) plan and kept the community firmly together. The Prophet used the time to pray intensely and pay homage to Allah (swt). His devotion and unwavering faith also strengthened the moral and spiritual resilience of the Muslims in the valley. They knew that Allah (swt) was on their side.

One day, when the Muslims were still holding out in the valley of Shi'b Abi Talib, Muhammad (saw) received a revelation that is recorded in the Holy Quran in Sura 29:2-3 (Al-Ankabut - The Spider):

Sura 29:2-3 (translated):
"Do people think they will be left alone just because they say: 'We believe' and that they will not be put to the test? We have tested those before them. And Allah will certainly make known those who speak the truth and will certainly make known the liars."

Allah (swt) revealed the verses to remind the believers that trials are an essential part of the path of faith and that they serve to test the steadfastness of faith.

After receiving the revelation, Muhammad (saw) called his followers together and shared the message with them. He explained to them the meaning of the verses and emphasized that the current trials and tribulations were part of a greater divine plan to test and strengthen the true faith of Muslims.

And the community also remained steadfast and supported each other. Even the Banu Hashim, including those who had not converted to Islam, stuck together and protected the Prophet Muhammad (saw) and his followers. Even some members of other clans among the Quraysh, who disagreed with the boycott, secretly helped the Muslims. They occasionally smuggled food and other necessary goods into the valley to alleviate some suffering.

The boycott finally ended after about three years through a combination of public pressure and internal tensions within the Quraysh. Some Meccans, including Hisham ibn Amr and Mut'im ibn Adi, who had previously smuggled food to the Muslims in the valley, expressed their displeasure at the injustice of the boycott. They argued that the measures were inhumane and therefore incompatible with the traditional values of the Quraysh.

There was also a remarkable incident that once again expressed the divine support of the Muslims. A turning point occurred when it was reported that termites had eaten away at the boycott document kept in the Ka'ba. Only the words "In the name of your Lord" remained intact. The Quraysh interpreted this as a divine sign that the boycott was unjust and should be ended.

The mixture of public pressure and the divine sign ultimately led to some high-ranking members of the Quraysh also calling for an end to the boycott.

Eventually, the leaders agreed to the lifting. After the decision was made, the supporters, including Hisham ibn Amr and Mut'im ibn Adi, went to the Ka`ba and removed the damaged document. They publicly declared that the boycott had been lifted and that the Muslims, the Banu Hashim, and Banu Muttalib, would be reintegrated into Meccan society. The Muslims, who had suffered under extreme conditions for over three years, were finally able to return to the city and take part in social and economic life.

In the year 619, Muhammad (saw) had to accept further blows of fate: the death of Abu Talib and Khadija (ra). When Muhammad (saw) began to preach Islam and experienced increasing hostility from the Quraysh, Abu Talib always stood firmly by his side. Although he did not abandon the pagan beliefs of his ancestors, he supported his nephew and protected him from the hostile Quraysh. Abu Talib's protection was crucial, as his position as one of the respected leaders of the tribe protected Muhammad (saw) from violence and persecution. When his uncle was dying, Muhammad (saw) desperately tried to convert him to Islam so that he could enter paradise. But Abu Talib refused and remained true to the faith of his ancestors. Despite his refusal to accept Islam, Abu Talib spoke words of support for Muhammad (saw) and his mission. The death of Abu Talib was a severe blow to Muhammad (saw) and the Muslim community. Without the protection of his influential uncle, Muhammad (saw) and his followers were even more exposed to the persecution of the Quraysh. Immediately after Abu Talib's death, hostility towards the Muslims in Mecca increased. The Quraysh took the opportunity to further harass Muhammad (saw) and his followers as they no longer had a powerful advocate.

Shortly after the death of Abu Talib, Khadija (ra) also passed away. The death of both so soon after each other was a profound loss for the Prophet, which hit him hard. Khadija (ra) was not only his first wife and the mother of his children but also his closest confidante and supporter since the beginning of his prophetic mission. This is why the year 619, a year of loss, is also known as "Am al-Huzn" (year of mourning).

Muhammad (saw) Meets the Other Prophets of Islam - The Night Journey and the Ascension (Isra and Mi'raj)

Two years after the death of Khadija (ra) and Abu Talib, in the year 621, Muhammad (saw) was to set out on an unusual and completely unexpected journey.

One night, he was visited by Jibril. The angel led Muhammad (saw) to an extraordinary, winged mount called Buraq and signaled the Prophet to mount it. On the back of Buraq, on which other prophets had already sat, Muhammad (saw) left Mecca flying and traveled to Jerusalem in a flash. Jibril accompanied him. In Jerusalem, they landed on the exact spot on the Temple Mount where the Al-Aqsa Mosque stands today. Then Jibril offered Muhammad (saw) a choice of three vessels. One contained water, one wine, and the other milk. Each drink symbolized different paths in life: water as a symbol of purity, wine for excess and drunkenness, and milk as a symbol of naturalness and purity.

Muhammad (saw) opted for the vessel of milk. This decision was deeply symbolic and showed his preference for purity and naturalness, paving the way for the ethical and moral foundations that would later be established in Islam. Then Jibrīl declared that Muhammad (saw) had made a wise decision. He turned to him and said: "Muhammad, you are rightly guided and so are your people. For wine is forbidden to you." This comment by Jibril pointed to the later Islamic rule prohibiting the consumption of alcohol.

After Muhammad (saw) drank the milk, he met the earlier prophets, from Adam (as) to Ibrâhîm (as), Mūsā (as) and ʿÎsa (as). They prayed together, with Muhammad (saw) leading the group in prayer. This emphasizes his role as the seal of the prophets in Islam, which means that he brings the final and complete revelation of Allah (swt).

After praying together, Muhammad (saw) continued the extraordinary journey known as Mi'raj. During this journey to the seven heavens, Muhammad (saw) was accompanied by Jibrīl.

In the first heaven, Muhammad (saw) met Adam, the first man and prophet. They exchanged greetings and blessings. Then Adam (as) took Muhammad (saw) on a deep spiritual journey in which he showed him the souls of his descendants. Adam (as) explained that he saw the souls of all the people who descended from him. These souls were divided into two groups: the souls of the believers and the souls of the unbelievers. The souls of the believers appeared on the right side of Adam (as). These souls shone with a radiant light that symbolized purity and virtue. They were in a state of peace and joy, which made Adam (as) happy. He smiled and blessed these souls, full of hope and pride in their righteousness and devotion to Allah (swt). On the left side of Adam (as) appeared the souls of the disbelievers. These souls were shrouded in darkness, representing the lack of faith. They seemed to be trapped in unrest and sorrow, which saddened Adam (as) greatly. Tears streamed down his face as he looked at the souls who had strayed from the path of Allah (swt). This vision that Adam (as) showed Muhammad (saw) was not only a revelation about the fate of mankind but also a valuable lesson about the consequences of belief and disbelief. It emphasized the importance of the prophetic mission of Muhammad (saw) and the need to guide people to the right path.

When they reached the second heaven, Muhammad (saw) met the prophets 'Īsa (as) and Yahyā (as). They greeted Muhammad (saw) warmly, and then they exchanged blessings. Isa (as) and Yahyā (as) also emphasized the centrality of the mission of Muhammad (saw). They declared that his message was the completion of the divine revelations that they had proclaimed. 'Īsa (as) emphasized that Muhammad (saw) was the last prophet whose arrival he had once predicted. Yahyā (as) supported these words and stressed the continuity of the prophetic messages. He explained that all prophets shared a common mission: to guide mankind, to call to the truth, and to proclaim Allah's (swt) commandments. He blessed Muhammad (saw) and encouraged him to remain steadfast in his mission, despite all the challenges and opposition he would face along the way.

In the third heaven, Muhammad (saw) met Yūsuf (as); the very Prophet known for his exceptional patience and virtue. Yūsuf (as), whose life story is often cited as an example of overcoming trials and a manifestation of divine justice, greeted Muhammad (saw) and shared a moment of spiritual exchange with him.

Then Muhammad (saw) and Jibrīl traveled to the fourth heaven, where Idrīs (as) was already waiting for them. Idrīs (as) is praised in the Quran for his wisdom and the interaction with him served to emphasize the importance of knowledge and wisdom in spiritual practice. In the fifth heaven, Muhammad (saw) met Hārūn (as), the brother and supporter of Mūsā (as). Their meeting emphasized the importance of brotherly support.

Muhammad (saw) and Jibril continued their journey and reached the sixth heaven. There they met Mūsā (as), one of the most revered prophets in the Islamic tradition. Their conversation was particularly profound; Mūsā (as) gave Muhammad (saw) important advice and spoke about the challenges faced by a prophet. The meeting between the Prophets Muhammad (saw) and

Mūsā (as) was one of the most significant moments of the Mi'raj and was to become particularly formative for Islamic prayer practice.

In the seventh heaven, the last and highest level, Muhammad (saw) met Ibrāhīm (as), the patriarch of the monotheistic religions. The meeting with Ibrāhīm (as) represented the universal dimension of faith that connects all Abrahamic religions. After this, Muhammad (saw) reached the highest point of his ascension. He reached the Sidrat al-Muntaha, a place considered the utmost limit and where the knowledge of creation ends. There, Muhammad (saw) experienced numerous visionary revelations. He received detailed insights into the hereafter. He saw the joys of paradise, where believers are rewarded for their virtue and righteousness. But he also saw the torments of hell, which are reserved for those who go against the commandments of Allah (swt).

Muhammad (saw) also met various angels who were stationed at the Sidrat al-Muntaha. These angels described to him their duties and roles in the universe, including overseeing the celestial realms and bestowing rewards and punishments on humans. Then, in this highest spiritual realm, Muhammad (saw) received confirmation of his prophetic mission and his role as the Seal of the Messengers. Allah (swt) confirmed that Muhammad (saw) was chosen to convey Islam's final and complete message.

At the Sidrat al-Muntaha, Muhammad (saw) finally received direct instruction from Allah (swt) to pray fifty times a day. This revelation of Allah (swt) was a direct divine instruction and represented a significant obligation for the Muslim community.

With this commandment of fifty daily prayers, Muhammad (saw) returned from the Sidrat al-Muntaha. On the way, he met Mūsā (as) again, who had a deep understanding of the practical aspects of the divine commandments through his many years of leadership experience with the Children of Israel, whom he had once led out of Egypt. Mūsā (as) was concerned. He felt that fifty prayers a day might be too demanding for the Ummah (Muslim religious community). He recommended that Muhammad (saw) return to Allah (swt) and ask for a reduction in the number of daily prayers. Muhammad (saw) accepted this advice. He turned to Allah (swt) in a sincere prayer and asked for alleviation of the burden on his community. In His mercy, the Almighty agreed to reduce the prayers to 40. But after Muhammad (saw) returned to Mūsā (as) and informed him that the number was still high, he recommended that he ask for further relief.

Muhammad (saw) listened to the advice of Mūsās (as) and asked Allah (swt) again for a further reduction. This dragged on until Allah (swt) limited the obligatory daily prayers to five, which He counted as 50 prayers. After the number of prayers had been set at five, Muhammad (saw) returned to Mūsā (as) and told him about it. Mūsā (as) again recommended that he ask for further reduction, but Muhammad (saw) decided that five prayers were appropriate.

Muhammad (saw) bid farewell to Mūsā (as), rode back to Jerusalem on the miraculous Mount Buraq, and then traveled to Mecca. The journey took place within a single night, but it was to leave its mark on Muhammad (saw) forever.

Immediately after his return, Muhammad (saw) shared his experiences with his followers and some of the Quraysh. For many of the believers, the story was a confirmation of their faith, and they were deeply impressed. Quickly, the details of the Isra and Mi'raj were spread among the Muslims, which further strengthened their faith and devotion to Allah (swt).

The Quraysh, on the other hand, reacted with disbelief and ridicule. They regarded the narrative as unbelievable. Some asked Muhammad (saw) to provide detailed descriptions of Jerusalem to verify his story. However,

Muhammad (saw) was able to provide these descriptions accurately, which made some of them ponder.

A remarkable incident in this context is the reaction of Abu Bakr. When the Quraysh told Abu Bakr (ra) about the journey, he replied without hesitation that he believed Muhammad (saw) because he trusted him in everything. Abu Bakr (ra) was then also called "As-Siddiq" (the truthful) because of his unwavering faith in the words of the Prophet.

However, the Quraysh's reactions to the reports of Muhammad (saw) further worsened tensions in Mecca. The rejection and mockery of the Meccan leaders led to increased persecution of the Muslims.

This period was a time of intense preparation and planning for the Hijrah, the emigration to Medina, which would ultimately mark the decisive turning point in the history of Islam. The Hijrah allowed Muslims to set up a new community and practice their faith freely, without the constant threat of the Quraysh.

Chapter

4

The Hijrah (Emigration to Medina)

The Hijrah, the emigration of the Prophet Muhammad (saw) and his followers from Mecca to Medina (then still Yathrib) in September 622, marks another decisive event in the history of Islam. This journey, which was not only spatial but spiritual, laid the foundation for the emergence of a new Muslim community and is counted in the Islamic calendar as the beginning of the Islamic era.

The Meetings of Aqaba

Initial plans and considerations to migrate to Yathrib (later Medina) existed before the Isra and Mi'raj. The decision to move to Yathrib was the result of a series of significant events and diplomatic efforts by the Prophet Muhammad (saw) and his followers. In the years before the Hijrah (emigration), Muhammad (saw) had already established contacts with some of the inhabitants of Yathrib. The city had been torn apart by internal tribal conflicts between the two main tribes, the Aws and the Khazraj. The conflicts had made the city unstable and many inhabitants of Yathrib were looking for a solution that could finally bring them peace and stability. At the same time, the persecution of Muslims in Mecca continued to increase, leaving them with no choice but to turn their backs on their hometown.

In 620, Muhammad (saw) met six men from the Khazraj tribe during the annual pilgrimage to Mecca. These men heard the message of Islam and embraced the faith. When they returned to Yathrib, they began to spread the teachings of Islam and gained new followers. The next year, in 621, twelve men from Yathrib came to Mecca and met Muhammad (saw) on the hill of Aqaba. These men belonged to the two rival tribes of Aws and Khazraj, each of which sent six representatives to Mecca. They sought guidance, peace, and new leadership. The men met Muhammad (saw) secretly on the hill of Aqaba, a place very close to Mecca. They were confident that Muhammad (saw) could help them resolve the ongoing conflicts in their hometown. The Prophet spoke to them about Islam and its teachings and offered them a prospect of peace and justice that could be achieved through faith in Allah (swt). The men from Yathrib listened intently to the wise words of Muhammad (saw) and finally gave him the so-called "Promise of Aqaba". They swore that they would never again practice idolatry, steal, commit fornication, kill children, or make false accusations and that they would obey the Prophet in all good things.

This promise was a significant milestone as it laid the foundation for the subsequent migration of Muslims to Yathrib and the formation of the first Muslim community outside Mecca. After the meeting, the twelve men returned to Yathrib and recounted what Muhammad (saw) had told them and their promise to him. Their goal was to gain more followers and spread the teachings of Islam in their hometown to restore peace and security to the city.

One year after the first meeting, in 622, a large group of around 75 people came to Mecca from Yathrib, including 73 men and two women. Many of them were already Muslims. They met again secretly with Muhammad (saw) on the hill of Aqaba. The Prophet emphasized that the strength of the Muslims lay in their unity and encouraged them to act as a united community, putting aside their differences and always supporting each other.

At this second meeting in Aqaba, the delegation from Yathrib invited Muhammad (saw) and the Muslims from Mecca to emigrate to their city. Muhammad (saw) turned directly to the men of Yathrib and asked, "Will you protect me as you protect your wives and children?" The leaders of the tribes replied unanimously that they would welcome and protect him and the Muslims coming from Mecca, even if it cost them their lives. These assurances were crucial, as they provided Muhammad (saw) and the Muslims from Mecca with the security and support they needed to emigrate to Yathrib.

So, after the second meeting in Aqaba, Muhammad (saw) and his followers began to plan the emigration. Muhammad (saw) instructed his followers to set out secretly in small groups so as not to attract the attention of the Quraysh. The Muslims gradually began to leave Mecca and gather in Yathrib, where the people warmly welcomed them. Muhammad (saw) initially stayed in Mecca.

The Murder Plot Against Muhammad (saw)

The Quraysh leaders, concerned about the growing number of emigrations, devised a plan to assassinate Muhammad (saw). They wanted to ensure that the Muslim movement would disintegrate without their leader. They met secretly in Dar an-Nadwa, the council and meeting house in Mecca, to discuss their plans. It was decided that each Quraysh family should choose a young, strong man from their ranks. The men were then to surround the Prophet's house together at night, attacking and killing him at the same time. In this way, the blame for his death was to be spread among all the tribes so that the Banu Hashim (the Prophet's clan) could not carry out an act of revenge against a single tribe.

After many Muslims were already on their way to Yathrib and the Quraysh began to intensify their persecution, Muhammad (saw) received a warning from Allah (swt) and the divine instruction to emigrate.

This revelation is mentioned in Sura 8:30 (Al-Anfal - The Booty):

Sura 8:30 (translated):
"And when those who disbelieved plotted against you to take you captive or to kill you or to drive you out. And they plotted, and Allah plotted, and Allah is the best of planners."

After the revelation, Muhammad (saw) prepared to leave Mecca. He informed Abu Bakr (ra) of the divine command to emigrate to Yathrib. On the night of the planned assassination, Ali ibn Abi Talib (ra), a cousin and loyal follower of the Prophet, slept in the Prophet's bed to deceive the conspirators and give Muhammad (saw) time to escape. While the Quraysh were keeping watch around the Prophet's house and Ali (ra) was in Muhammad's (saw) bed, Muhammad (saw) slipped out unnoticed. He recited the verse from Sura 36:9 (Ya-Sin), which reads as follows:

This recitation protected him from the eyes of the conspirators, and he was able to reach Abu Bakr's (ra) house safely. Abu Bakr (ra) had already prepared everything for their secret departure. He organized camels and ensured the two had enough provisions for the journey. Together Muhammad (saw) and Abu Bakr left for Yathrib under the cover of darkness. To deceive the Quraysh, who would probably pursue them, they first took a different route and traveled to a cave on Mount Thaur. They planned to stay in the cave for some time before continuing their journey. They also sent some camels in the opposite direction intending to deceive the Quraish and lure them onto a false trail.

Even before they arrived at the cave, they left their camels in the care of Amir ibn Fuhayrah, a shepherd and former slave of Abu Bakr (ra) and an early follower of Islam. The two men eventually reached a cave on Mount Thaur and spent three days and nights there while the Meccans searched feverishly for them. When the two men entered the cave, a spider rushed up and spun a large web at the entrance. Then a dove began to nest right at the entrance to the cave. Thanks to this divine intervention and the protection of Allah (swt), it seemed as if the cave had been abandoned and had not been entered by humans for a long time. Even when the pursuers stood in front of the cave, they had no idea that Muhammad (saw) and Abu Bakr (ra) were hiding in it. There were no footprints to be seen in the sand either, as the faithful Amir covered the tracks by driving his sheep across the entrance to the cave.

But Muhammad (saw) and Abu Bakr (ra) received further help. Abu Bakr's (ra) son, Abd Allah, provided news from Mecca at night. The information about the actions of the Quraysh was crucial in deciding the right time to continue their journey and to ensure that they chose routes not watched by the Meccans. Abu Bakr's daughter, the then 28-year-old Asma (ra), also helped them. She brought them something to eat and drink in the cave. She also prepared food parcels to protect the food from the heat and sand on the arduous journey through the desert. Asma (ra), who was very clever and far-sighted, quickly found a practical solution to transport the provisions safely. She reached for her belt, a simple piece of cloth she wore around her waist, and tore it in two. She carefully tied the food parcels and the water hose together with these parts of her belt.

On the third night, Abd Allah brought news that the Quraysh's search was slowly subsiding. So, Muhammad (saw) and Abu Bakr (ra) ventured out of their hiding place and continued their journey to Medina. The camels picked them up from a meeting point previously arranged with Amir and set off.

The two paid a trustworthy desert guide named Abdullah ibn Urayqit, who knew the ways of the desert well and had the task of guiding them safely to Medina. Abdullah led Muhammad (saw) and Abu Bakr (ra) on a route that few people knew, and was considerably longer than the direct route from Mecca to Yathrib. Nevertheless, the route was safer as it was less monitored. The desert guide's ability to navigate them through the difficult terrain of the Arabian Peninsula was crucial to reaching their destination. His knowledge of water sources and hiding places in the desert helped them to survive the journey unscathed despite the extreme conditions and the constant threat from the Quraysh. They braved the scorching heat during the day and the cold of the desert at night.

But further dangers were to lie in wait for them. Suraqa ibn Malik was a resident of Mecca who, lured by the reward offered by the Quraysh for the capture of Muhammad (saw), decided to take up the pursuit on his own. As an experienced tracker, Suraqa believed that he would easily track down Muhammad (saw) and Abu Bakr (ra), hand them over to the Quraysh, and collect the generous reward himself. So, well equipped and on horseback, he set off in pursuit, guided by the clues he had gathered in Mecca about the possible whereabouts of the fugitives. He was not fooled by the false trail, quickly caught up, and came close to Muhammad (saw), Abu Bakr (ra), and Abdullah.

But the closer he got to the fugitives, the more difficult the journey became, because Allah (swt) supported Muhammad (saw) and his companions. Suraqa's horse sank into the sand several times, even though the ground seemed firm. He feared that he would not make any further progress so deep did his horse sink and he had to use all his strength to move forward.

When he finally approached them and had direct visual contact with Muhammad (saw), something extraordinary happened: Muhammad (saw) spoke to him and gave him a prophecy. He told Suraqa that if he stopped the persecution, he would be rewarded handsomely and one day he would wear the bracelets of the Persian emperor. Suraqa was confused and this prophecy seemed unbelievable to him at first, but it left a lasting impression on him. The prophecy, paired with the divine signs he experienced during his persecution brought about an immediate and lasting change in Suraqa. He recognized the truthfulness of Muhammad (saw) and the importance of his mission. Suraqa stopped his persecution and was to convert to Islam a few years later. The prophecy was also fulfilled remarkably when Suraqa wore the bracelets of the Persian emperor Khusro after the Muslims had conquered Persia - but one by one.

The Stay in Quba and the Construction of the First Mosque

Since their departure from the cave on Mount Thaur near Mecca, Muhammad (saw), Abu Bakr (ra), and Abdullah had been traveling for about seven days. Then, on 8 Rabi' al-Awwal (September 23, 622), they finally reached Quba, a suburb about five kilometers south of Yathrib. There they were warmly welcomed by the inhabitants, who gave them water and something to eat.

Muhammad (saw) and his companion Abu Bakr (ra) decided to stay in Quba for a while. There were several important reasons for this decision. Of course, they first wanted to recover from the hardships of the arduous journey and gather new strength. In addition, the Prophet wanted to ensure the safety of the other Muslim emigrants (Muhajirun) from Mecca who were also on their way to Yathrib. By waiting in Quba, he could check whether all the Muslims traveling in small groups had survived the dangerous journey and no one had been left behind. The stopover in Quba made it possible to gather the stragglers and unite the Muslim community before they set off together for Yathrib. Among the stragglers was Ali ibn Abi Talib (ra), Muhammad's (saw) cousin, who had stayed behind in Mecca to carry out certain tasks. He was to ensure that no personal possessions and valuables entrusted to him were left behind and fell into the hands of the Quraysh. He also ensured that the rest of the Muslims in Mecca could follow safely to Yathrib.

Muhammad (saw) and his followers used their time in Quba to build a mosque that would serve as a place of prayer and assembly for the community in

Quba. The construction of the Quba Mosque, which has gone down in history as Islam's first house of worship, only took about a week - after all, everyone pitched in and could rely on the support of the Almighty. (See 1. on map 3)

Muslims gathered regularly to pray and meditate together with Muhammad (saw). These were days of spiritual strengthening and mutual support.

The Entry of Muhammad (saw) into Yathrib

When more Muslims finally arrived in Quba from Mecca, Muhammad (saw) and his companions decided to set off for Yathrib. The community, which had now grown to several dozen Muslims, set off for Yathrib.

Muhammad (saw) rode on his camel, accompanied by Abu Bakr (ra) and the other Muslims. The departure was done in a solemn and orderly manner, with the Muslims going in groups to ensure an organized procession to Yathrib.

When they arrived in the city, they were greeted with joy and respect by the Muslims living there and the tribes of the city. The Muslims from Yathrib, the Ansar (helpers) who had previously expressed their support and faith in Muhammad (saw) at the Aqaba meetings, as well as the Muhajirun (emigrants) who were already there, came together to welcome Muhammad (saw), Abu Bakr (ra), Ali (ra) and the other stragglers. Children and adults sang songs of joy and hope. It is reported that people sang "Tala'a al-Badru 'Alayna", a song that is still sung on festive Islamic occasions, to celebrate the Prophet's arrival. This song expresses the deep love and respect that the people of Yathrib felt for Muhammad (saw).

Tala'a al-Badru 'Alayna:

Original Arabic text:

طلع البدر علينا

من ثنيات الوداع

وجب الشكر علينا

ما دعا لله داع

أيها المبعوث فينا

جئت بالأمر المطاع

جئت شرفت المدينة

مرحباً يا خير داع

Appropriate German translation:

The full moon has risen over us
from the Valley of Peace
and it is our duty to show gratitude

As long as someone in existence calls out to God
O our messenger among us
Who has come with words of admonition to be heeded
You have brought purity to this city
Welcome you, who calls us to a good path

Phonetic transcription (German):

Tala'a al-Badru 'Alayna,
Min Thaniyyat al-Wada'
Wajab ash-Shukru 'Alayna,
Ma Da'a Li-Ilahi Da'

Ayyuha al-Mab'uthu Fina,
Ji'ta bi-l-Amri al-Muta'
Ji'ta Sharafta al-Madina,
Marhaban Ya Khaira Da'

Retrieve QR code to play Tala'a al-Badru 'Alayna:

https://qrfy.io/p/nnEZtzzb9x

Muhammad (saw) had his camel, Qaswa, decide where he and his family would live in the future. The camel finally stopped at a piece of land owned by two orphan boys. The brothers, Sahl and Suhayl, had inherited the piece of land from their deceased father Amr. Muhammad (saw) called the guardians of the orphan boys and offered to buy the land. Although the guardians and the community offered to give the land to the Prophet, Muhammad (saw) insisted on paying the full price - out of deep respect for the property of others, especially orphans. Muhammad (saw) bought the land and decided to build his house and the future Prophet's Mosque on it.

Chapter 5

Life in Medina

Shortly after Muhammad (saw) arrived in Yathrib, people increasingly began to refer to the city as "Madinat an-Nabi" (City of the Prophet) or "al-Madīna" for short.

Construction of the Prophet's Mosque began immediately after being bought and upon the arrival of Muhammad (saw) and his companions in Medina in 622, shortly after the Hijrah. The Prophet himself took an active part in the construction of the mosque. He carried stones and building materials and showed by his example the importance of community work and commitment. The Prophet's companions, including well-known personalities such as Abu Bakr (ra) and Ali (ra), also participated in the construction. They worked side by side with the Ansar and the Muhajirun.

The Prophet's Mosque quickly became the center of religious, social, and political life for the Muslim community in Medina. It served as a place of prayer and a meeting place for the shura (consultation), the school, and the court. Muhammad (saw) also used the mosque for political and strategic decision-making.

The Establishment of the First Islamic State by the Prophet Muhammad (saw)

After arriving in Medina and while the Prophet's Mosque was still being built in 622, Muhammad (saw) began to establish an Islamic state that would serve as a model for later Muslim communities.

The Ansar played a central role in building this new Islamic community in Medina. Not only did they share their homes and resources with the Muhajirun, but they also stood firmly by the Prophet Muhammad (saw) in defending the fledgling community against external threats and in expanding the influence of Islam. The solidarity between the Muhajirun and the Ansar is often cited as a model example of Islamic brotherhood and mutual support. Muhammad's (saw) and Abu Bakr's (ra) arrival in the city thus marked not only the end of their flight but the beginning of a new era of Islam.

This state, which Muhammad (saw) began to establish, was based on the principles of Sharia, the divine laws defined by the revelations of the Quran and the Sunnah (the practice established and confirmed by the Prophet). Shortly after he arrived in Medina, Allah (swt) revealed to His Prophet guidelines that served as the basis for the Document of Medina and constituted the foundation of the Islamic legal system (Sharia) that is still in use today. The Medina Document is also known as the Constitution of Medina and the "Sahifah". This document was also a formal pact between the Muhajirun, the Ansar, and the Jewish tribes. It laid down the principles of coexistence and mutual support.

There have been several revelations related to the principles and guidelines of the Medina Document. These revelations emphasize the importance of justice, unity, and the protection of the Muslim community.

Thus, Sura 49:10 (Al-Hujurat - The Chambers) was revealed to Muhammad (saw) by Allah (swt):

Sura 49:10 (translated):
"The believers are brothers. So, make peace between your two brothers and fear Allah so that you may find mercy."

This revelation served as the basis for unity and brotherhood within the Muslim community. It ensured that all members of the community considered themselves brothers and encouraged them to resolve conflicts peacefully. The Medina Document thus included the promotion of peace and unity among the believers, which was essential for the stability of the young Muslim society.

Allah (swt) also revealed Sura 3:103 (Aal-Imran - the clan of Imran) to his Prophet:

Sura 3:103 (translated):
"And hold fast to Allah's rope together and do not separate. And remember the favor of Allah that He bestowed on you when you were enemies, and He joined your hearts together so that you became brothers by His favor. And you were on the edge of a pit of fire, and He saved you from it. So, Allah makes His signs clear to you so that you may be guided."

Adherence to Allah's (swt) rope symbolizes adherence to the faith and Islamic principles that strengthen the community. In the context of the Medina Document, this encouraged Muslims to overcome their differences and act as a united Ummah (community).

In addition, Muhammad (saw) received instructions from Allah (swt) that emphasized the importance of justice and righteousness, such as Sura 4:58 (An-Nisa - The Women):

Sura 4:58 (translated):
"Allah commands you to return the goods entrusted to you to their owners and, when you judge between people, to judge with justice. How excellent is that with which Allah admonishes you! For Allah is All-Hearing and All-Seeing."

The Medina Document incorporated these principles to ensure that all members of the community were treated fairly, and that the administration of justice was based on equity and equality.

In Sura 5:8 (Al-Ma'idah - The Tablet), revealed by Allah (swt), Muslims are asked to always be just, regardless of personal feelings or prejudices. This was an important aspect of the Medina document, which emphasized the need to always be just.

Sura 5:8 (translated):
"O you who believe, be persistent in standing up for Allah

> *as witnesses for righteousness. And do not let hatred of people prevent you from being righteous. Be righteous, that is closer to the fear of Allah. And fear Allah. Allah knows what you do."*

In addition, Allah (swt) established rules for the defense and protection of the Muslim community, which He revealed to His Prophet, and which are recorded in the Holy Quran in Sura 22:39-40 (Al-Hajj - The Pilgrimage):

> **Sura 22:39-40 (translated):**
> **"Permission (to fight) is given to those who are fought because they have been wronged - and indeed Allah has the power to help them - (to those) who have been driven out of their homes guiltlessly just because they say, 'Our Lord is Allah. And if Allah did not reject some people by means of others, monasteries, churches, synagogues, and mosques in which Allah's name is frequently mentioned would certainly have been destroyed. And Allah will surely help those who help Him. Indeed, Allah is Strong and Almighty."**

These verses allowed Muslims to defend themselves against injustice and persecution. In the Medina Document, this was included as a legal basis for the collective defense of the community against external threats, such as the Quraysh.

Not to be forgotten are the revelations that emphasize freedom of religious choice and tolerance towards those of other faiths, such as Sura 2:256 (Al-Baqarah - The Cow) and Sura 60:8 (Al-Mumtahina - The Test).

Sura 2:256 (translated):
"There is no compulsion in faith. The rightful has now become clear compared to the wrongdoing. Therefore, whoever renounces the Taghut (false gods, unrighteous rulers, or tyrannical powers) and believes in Allah, he has grasped the firmest handhold in which there is no tearing. And Allah is All-Hearing and All-Knowing."

Revelation emphasizes freedom of belief and makes it clear that no one should be forced to adopt a religion. In the Medina document, this was integrated to ensure that all religious groups within the city - Muslims, Jews, and polytheists - could live together peacefully.

Sura 60:8 (translated):
"Allah does not forbid you to be kind to those who have not fought against you for the sake of religion and have not driven you out of your homes, and to treat them justly. Indeed, Allah loves the righteous."

This revelation of Allah (swt) emphasizes the need to be kind and just to those who neither fight nor expel Muslims. In the Document of Medina, this was laid down as a principle of peaceful coexistence and fair treatment of all inhabitants of the city, regardless of their faith.

All parties who signed the Medina Document pledged to protect each other from external enemies and at the same time to settle internal conflicts peacefully. Each group also had the right to practice their religion freely and it was made clear that Muslims and Jews would regulate their religious affairs independently of each other. In addition, each group was to administer justice according to its laws and traditions, if these did not contradict the overriding principles of the constitution. Among the most important groups that were part of this alliance were the two major Ansar tribes: the Aws and the Khazraj, as well as the Jewish tribes. These had long been rivals, but under Muhammad's (saw) leadership they were united into a single Muslim community. To further strengthen the unity between the Muhajirun and the Ansar, Muhammad (saw) had an excellent idea: he introduced the system of brotherhood. Each Muhajir was assigned to an Ansar to create a deep personal and economic bond.

Faced with the threat of the Meccan Quraysh and other hostile tribes, Muhammad (saw) organized the defense of Medina by forming a well-organized military structure. This included training Muslims for battle, setting up security patrols, and devising elaborate plans to defend the city from attackers.

But that was by no means all that Muhammad (saw) did to strengthen the young Muslim community in Medina. The Prophet also made a decisive contribution to agricultural development in and around the city, which significantly improved the food supply and led to economic independence.

Of course, Muhammad (saw) was aware that allies are of great value. For this reason, he actively sought diplomatic relations with various tribes and groups in the Arabian Peninsula. He made treaties and alliances to expand the influence of the Muslim community and resolve potential conflicts peacefully. This strategy helped decisively in the spread of the Muslim faith in the region and beyond.

Muhammad (saw) also recognized the strategic necessity of establishing peaceful relations with the Bedouin tribes around Medina. Through a series of treaties and agreements, he secured the Muslims the support or at least the neutrality of these tribes. These allies were particularly important for securing supply routes and establishing a line of defense against possible attacks from Mecca.

Something very significant also happened in spiritual terms. The official direction of prayer (qibla) prescribed for Muslims was changed. Previously, Muhammad (saw) often looked up to the sky and wished to change the Qibla towards the Ka`ba in Mecca. This wish of the Prophet was finally granted. For when Muhammad (saw) and his companions were engrossed in prayer, Allah (swt) revealed Sura 2:144 (Al-Baqara - The Cow) through the angel Jibrīl:

Sura 2:144 (translated):
"We often see your face turned towards the sky.
Therefore, We will surely turn you in a direction of prayer
that pleases you. So, turn your face towards the Sacred
Mosque (Ka'ba). And wherever you (believers) are, turn
your faces in its direction. Those who have been given the
Book surely know that this is the truth from their Lord.
And Allah is not heedless of what they do."

Muhammad (saw) was very happy about this and since then Muslims have prayed towards the Ka'ba in Mecca and no longer towards Jerusalem.

The Battle of Badr

Muhammad's (saw) preparations to militarize and defend Medina had paid off. The first battle that Muhammad (saw) and the Muslims had to fight was imminent. In the Battle of Badr, the young Muslim community had to assert itself against the Meccans under the leadership of the Quraysh. The battle took place on the 17th of Ramadan of the year 2 after the Hijrah, which corresponds to March 13th of the year 624, near the well of Badr and therefore bears its name. (See 4. on map 1) It is one of the most famous and important battles in early Islamic history.

The Quraysh from Mecca continued to view the emerging Islam and its followers as a threat to their influence and economic interests. In Medina, on the other hand, the Muslims were looking for ways to strengthen their economy. A key aspect of this was the interception of trade caravans on the routes linking Mecca with Syria, which were controlled by the Quraysh. At the beginning of the year 624, Muhammad (saw) learned of a particularly valuable caravan traveling back to Mecca from Syria under the leadership of Abu Sufyan. The Muslims saw this as a good opportunity both to compensate for the financial losses they had suffered by leaving their old homeland and to weaken the Quraysh.

Abu Sufyan, whose full name was Sakhr ibn Harb, was a successful and respected merchant and belonged to the Quraysh tribe. He held a high position within the ranks of the Quraysh and led many trade caravans, including those that sought to intercept Muhammad (saw) and the other Muslims. Thanks to the spies the Quraysh had among the Muslims, the caravan leader learned of the Muslims' plans. He quickly changed the route of the caravan and at the same time sent messengers back to Mecca to request reinforcements. The Quraysh, alarmed and determined to defend their economic interests and pride, quickly mobilized a large force. Around 1000 armed warriors set out to confront and crush the Muslims.

Muhammad (saw) and his followers, about 313 men, mostly ill-equipped and significantly outnumbered, set out to confront the Meccan superiority. Despite their numerical inferiority, the Muslims were highly motivated and knew they could rely on the Prophet's wise strategic decisions and Allah's (swt) aid, even though they were outnumbered.

The first important decision that the military leader Muhammad (saw) made was the choice of battlefield. He decided to confront the Meccan troops at the wells of Badr, which gave the Muslims some strategic advantages. Muhammad (saw) had his troops occupy the few wells in the vicinity. This, in turn, caused problems for the Quraysh, as they had to supply their fighters with water, which was now much more difficult. In addition, the Muslims positioned themselves so that they had a good view of their enemies without being directly exposed to the sunlight. The Quraysh, on the other hand, stood against the sun and were blinded, which severely impaired their vision and fighting ability.

Moreover, the Prophet motivated his fighters before and during the battle through powerful speeches in which he emphasized the importance of their fight and highlighted the divine support. He repeatedly assured them they were fighting for their righteous cause and that Allah (swt) was firmly at their side.

The confrontation at the Battle of Badr began with individual duels, which were customary to demonstrate the strength and courage of the best fighters. Muhammad's (saw) cousin, Ali ibn Abi Talib (ra), and Muhammad's (saw) Uncle, Hamza ibn Abdul-Muttalib (ra), were among those who fought in these early duels and defeated their Quraysh challengers. After other leading Quraysh fighters, including figures such as Walid ibn Utbah, also fell in the duels, the tension increased. The death of the leaders had a demoralizing effect on the Quraysh and a motivating effect on the Muslims.

Then the actual battle began. The Prophet Muhammad (saw) gathered a handful of pebbles beforehand and threw them in the direction of the enemy Quraysh while saying: "May their faces be disfigured!" This is mentioned in the Quran (Sura 8:17) and symbolizes the beginning of the great battle.

The Muslims launched a concentrated attack against the Meccan forces, supported by their strong faith and martial discipline. The Quraysh were led by Amr ibn Hisham, better known as Abu Jahl, still one of the fiercest opponents of Muhammad (saw). Despite the misgivings of other Quraysh leaders, such as Abu Sufyan, Abu Jahl insisted on confronting the Muslims.

During the heated battle of Badr, two young Muslims, Muadh ibn Amr and Muawwadh ibn Afra, recognized Abu Jahl on the battlefield. They attacked him together. Both were determined to defeat him. The traditions describe how the two of them severely wounded Abu Jahl. After Abu Jahl fell to the ground, another companion of the Prophet Muhammad (saw), Abdullah ibn Mas'ud (ra), found him. With a coup de grace, he killed the badly wounded enemy. But the Quraysh were still clearly outnumbered.

Given this superiority of the enemies of the Muslims, divine intervention took place. In Sura 8:9-10 (Al-Anfal - The Booty) it says:

Sura 8:9-10 (translated):
"When you called upon your Lord for help, He answered you: "I will support you with a thousand angels riding in succession." And Allah made this only as good news for

you and so that your hearts would find peace through it. Victory comes only from Allah. Indeed, Allah is All-Powerful, All-Wise."

The angels appeared in white robes and rode on large, white horses. They actively fought against the Quraysh and contributed to their chaos and demoralization.

The Muslims saw the heads of the enemies being cut off by invisible blades. No one doubted that this was the work of the angels sent by Allah (swt). In the Holy Quran in Sura 8:12 (Al-Anfal - The Booty) is the instruction Allah (swt) gave to the angels.

Sura 8:12 (translated):
"When your Lord told the angels, 'I am with you, so strengthen those who believe. I will strike terror into the hearts of those who disbelieve. Strike their necks and cut off every finger!"

In addition, some companions reported that they had extraordinary powers in the battle of Badr that they could not explain. They fought faster and better than they normally could, which was attributed to the direct support of Allah (swt).

The Quraysh, taken by surprise by the unexpected strength of the Muslims and the losses of many of their leaders, were finally overwhelmed and put to flight.

The Battle of Badr thus ended with a clear victory for the Muslims. This victory had far-reaching consequences for both sides: It significantly strengthened the moral and political position of the Prophet Muhammad (saw) and was also a decisive moment in the establishment of Islam as a significant force in the Arabian Peninsula. The fallen Muslims received immediate access to paradise as martyrs, as stated in the Holy Quran in Sura 3:169 (Aal-Imran - the clan of Imran):

Sura 3:169 (translated):
"And do not think that those who are killed in the way of Allah are dead. No, they are alive and will be provided for by their Lord."

For the Quraysh, the defeat was a severe blow that led to a reorganization of their leadership structure and a reassessment of their strategy towards the Muslims.

Many of the leading members had been killed, including key figures such as Abu Jahl, which left a huge gap in the political and military leadership of the Quraysh. The Quraysh were forced to reconsider their earlier underestimation of the Muslim community and to take the threat of Muhammad (saw) and his followers more seriously. The surviving Quraysh leaders, including Abu Sufyan, who gained increasing political influence in Mecca, began to plan and carry out more targeted measures against the Muslims. The direct military confrontation at Badr had proved disastrous, so the Quraysh changed their tactics to make better use of their resources and strategic advantages. This included setting up increased trade blockades against Medina and forming new alliances with other Arab tribes to create a broader resistance to the spread of Islam.

The Prophet Muhammad (saw) and his followers returned triumphantly to Medina after the surprising and decisive victory in the Battle of Badr. There the remaining Muslims jubilantly greeted them. The victory had far-reaching consequences, both within the Muslim community and in their relationship with the surrounding tribes.

The return to Medina marked the beginning of a new phase in which Muhammad (saw) cemented his claim to leadership and influenced the social and political structures of the city. The Prophet used his strengthened position to expand the Islamic legal system, by gradually introducing decrees and laws. These were intended to regulate various aspects of life, such as family, criminal, economic, and social law.

For family law, important provisions on marriage, divorce, inheritance, and family obligations were introduced. The provisions on marriage in Islamic law included clear instructions on marriage, which required the consent of both parties. The Prophet (saw) also introduced regulations that ensured the proper treatment of wives and protected the rights of women in marriage. This included the stipulation of a suitable bridal gift (mahr) to be given by the groom to the bride as a sign of financial commitment.

Allah (swt) revealed this in Sura 4:4 (An-Nisa - The Women)

Sura 4:4 (translated):
"And give the women their morning gift (bridal gift) as a voluntary gift. But if they give you some of it of their own accord, enjoy it as wholesome and pleasant."

Marriage was seen as a contractual union that entailed both legal and moral obligations for both spouses.

There were also some important changes in criminal law; one of the most significant involved theft. The Quran stipulates severe punishments for thieves set out in Sura 5:38 (Al-Ma'idah - The Tablet).

> Sura 5:38 (translated):
> "Cut off the hand of the thief and the thief as a reward for what they have committed - a deterrent from Allah. Allah is All-Powerful and All-Wise."

So, it was ordered that a thief's hand should be cut off, but only under strict conditions of proof and circumstances designed to prevent abuse of the law. This measure was aimed at ensuring the sanctity of personal property. Specific rules were also laid down for murder and manslaughter, which Allah (swt) revealed to Muhammad (saw), and which can be found in Sura 2:178 (Al-Baqara - The Cow) in the Holy Quran, among other places.

> Sura 2:178 (translated):
> "O believers! The law of retribution is laid down for you in the case of murder - a free man for a free man, a slave for a slave, and a woman for a woman. But if the perpetrator is pardoned by the victim's patron, then the blood money should be decided fairly, and payment should be made courteously. This is a concession and a mercy from your

The Quran therefore stipulates that murders can be avenged, i.e., that qisas (retribution) against the murderer is allowed. However, it is also possible for the victim's family to accept blood money (diya) and forgive the perpetrator.

Fornication was another serious offense that Muhammad (saw) regulated within the framework of criminal law. The revelations he received after the Battle of Badr stipulated severe punishments for this. If this was proven, the punishments provided were very severe. Traditionally, these included flogging. Allah (swt) revealed this to Muhammad (saw) in Sura 24:2 (An-Nur - The Light).

Sura 24:2 (translated):
"The lewd and the lewd - give each of them a hundred lashes, and do not let pity for them overcome you in Allah's religion, if you believe in Allah and the Last Day. And let a group of believers witness their punishment."

According to the traditions in the hadiths, fornication or adultery committed by married persons meant stoning to death. These punishments were intended as a deterrent to preserve the integrity of families. In cases of adultery without full proof, direct physical punishment was not applicable. Instead, a public reprimand was issued. This could take the form of warnings or social disapproval by the community. The aim of this was to make the person concerned repent and correct their behavior, but without applying the extreme punishments that were intended for proven adultery.

Not to be forgotten are the principles that the Prophet Muhammad (saw) introduced to ensure justice in dealing with people accused of crimes. These included the strict prohibition of torture and ill-treatment to force confessions.

To strengthen the economic stability of Medina, Muhammad (saw) promoted trade and set up fair trade practices that would prevent fraud and promote fair business. These practices were not only to ensure economic prosperity but also to reflect the social and moral values of Islam. Thus, Muhammad (saw) emphasized the importance of honesty and transparency in trading. He taught his followers that they should disclose all relevant information when selling goods. This included the prohibition of concealing defects or making false statements about the quality or origin of products. The Prophet also warned very strongly of the severe consequences of usury, both in this world and in the hereafter.

Islam prohibits interest (riba), which is considered unjust, especially if it leads to excessive debt and economic exploitation. This prohibition can be traced back to revelations that Muhammad (saw) received from Allah (swt). It is written in Sura 2:275 (Al-Baqara - The Cow) in the Holy Quran.

Sura 2:275 (translated):
"Those who take interest will stand no other than as one whom Satan has struck down by madness. This is because they say, 'Trading is the same as taking interest. But Allah has permitted trading and forbidden taking interest. So, whoever receives an admonition from his Lord, and stops,

Therefore, Muhammad (saw) encouraged alternative forms of financing and lending to ensure that transactions served the financial stability and welfare of the community.

He also acted against the formation of monopolies and encouraged retailers to set fair prices. He disapproved of practices in which merchants colluded with each other to inflate prices. At that time, it was common in trade to emphasize the quality or value of a product by swearing to it. Muhammad (saw) taught his followers that false swearing or lying is a sin and ultimately diminishes the blessing of a transaction (barakah).

The Prophet also adjusted social law. Muhammad (saw) had always emphasized the importance of mutual support. When Sura 2:177 (Al-Baqara - The Cow) was finally revealed to him by Allah (swt), the Prophet introduced Zakat.

Sura 2:177 (translated):
"Piety does not consist in turning your faces towards the East or the West. But piety consists in believing in Allah and the Last Day and the angels and the Book and the prophets and giving money - though you love it - to your relatives and the orphans and the needy and the traveler and the supplicant and for the liberation of slaves, and

Zakat is a charitable levy, a form of alms tax, which aims to redistribute wealth within the Muslim community and promote social justice. At the same time, zakat is one of the five pillars of Islam. The traditional zakat rate is 2.5 % of saved assets as soon as a certain minimum wealth (nisab) is exceeded. This tax is used to support the needy, including the poor, those burdened by debt and travelers.

The Battle of Uhud

In the meantime, however, the enemies of the emerging Muslim community did not sleep but prepared for their vendetta against Muhammad (saw), Islam and his followers. After the defeat at the Battle of Badr, the Quraysh were eager to restore their lost honor, secure their trade routes and expand their power.

Led by Abu Sufyan, the Quraysh mobilized a large force. The wounds of defeat were deep, and the Meccan elite was determined to strike a decisive blow against Muhammad (saw) and his followers.

In 625, around a year after the Battle of Badr, the Quraysh mobilized an army of around 3,000 fighters. This included cavalry and foot soldiers, equipped with the best weapons and armor. This force was considerably larger and better equipped than the troops they had sent to Badr at the time. So, the Quaraysh warriors marched to Medina. The march of the troops from Mecca was not a surprise attack, as the Muslims had seen the movements of the Meccan army and had time to prepare for the impending confrontation. As soon as the Prophet Muhammad (saw) learned of the troop movements, he held a war council. He wanted to discuss the best course of action with his followers. While some of the older Sahaba (companions of the Prophet) pleaded to stay in the city and defend it, the younger Muslims urged him to leave Medina and face the Quraysh in open battle. Muhammad (saw) decided to listen to the opinion of the majority. He led his forces out of the city to face the Quraysh on Mount Uhud, about eleven kilometers from the city gates of Medina. (See 2. on map 3)

The Muslim army, consisting of around 700 fighters, positioned itself with its back to Mount Uhud. Muhammad (saw) deliberately chose this strategic position to avoid a direct confrontation near the city and to protect his troops from an attack from behind. The Prophet then instructed 50 archers under the command of Abdullah ibn Jubayr to occupy a small hill called Jabal ar-Rumma, which was considered a key position for securing the flanks of the small army. Muhammad (saw) gave direct orders to Abdullah ibn Jubayr not to leave their position under any circumstances to protect the Muslim army from possible Quraysh evasion maneuvers.

Nevertheless, despite the clear instructions of Muhammad (saw), the prospect of rich booty tempted some archers to abandon their posts. When the Quraysh troops began to flee under the pressure of Muslim attacks, leaving their camps and equipment seemingly unprotected, many archers saw the opportunity to enrich themselves. The booty consisted not only of the weapons and armor left behind by the Quraysh, but also other valuables that represented an attractive financial reward for the fighters. In the heat of battle and corrupted by the opportunity for easy pickings, they abandoned their strategic position on the hill.

The archers' decision opened a critical gap in the Muslim defense. Khalid ibn al-Walid, then still a leader of the Meccan cavalry and later one of the most famous Muslim generals, recognized the opportunity. With a group of cavalrymen, he led a quick and decisive flanking attack through the now unprotected gap. This tactical move allowed the Quraysh to attack the Muslim forces from behind, causing confusion, confusion, and many casualties.

The battle, which until then had gone in favor of the Muslims, quickly turned into a chaotic slaughter that ended in death for many Muslims.

Hamza ibn Abdul-Muttalib (ra), the Prophet's uncle, who had already fought in the Battle of Badr and struck down many of his opponents, also died at the foot of Mount Uhud. Hamza (ra), known as the "Lion of Allah", was deliberately killed. An Abyssinian slave of the Quraysh named Wahshi ibn Harb killed Hamza (ra) in an insidious manner. He was instigated to do so by Hind bint Utbah, the wife of Abu Sufyan and one of the most prominent Quraysh women. She promised him freedom if he killed Hamza (ra). Hind harbored a special grudge against Hamza (ra) because he had killed her father, brother, and uncle at the Battle of Badr, whereupon she swore revenge. Wahshi, an excellent spear thrower, later described how he watched Hamza (ra) on the battlefield and waited for the right moment to strike. With all his strength, he hurled his spear at Hamza (ra) as he was fighting with another Meccan warrior. The spear struck Hamza (ra) with such force that he was mortally wounded. Wahshi then withdrew and waited until the fight subsided. He then sought the body as evidence for Hind to gain his freedom. Hind bint Utbah then ordered her slave Wahshi ibn Harb to mutilate Hamza's (ra) body. So Wahshi cut out Hamza's (ra) liver and brought it to Hind, who then tried to eat it. However, she failed and threw up. In some traditions, this is seen as a sign of divine intervention, meaning that Allah (swt) did not allow Hamza (ra) to be dishonored in this way. But then Hind cut off Hamza's (ra) ears and nose and turned them into necklaces and bracelets. This cruel act of revenge illustrates the heinousness of their actions and was considered extremely barbaric by Muslims.

Even the Prophet was directly involved in the fighting and was injured in the heat of battle. A stone thrown by a Meccan warrior hit him in the head. The force of the impact pushed his helmet against his head, causing two of the chainmail rings to dig deep into his cheek. The prophet also lost two of his teeth. Although these injuries were painful and bled profusely, they were not life-threatening. The Prophet's direct involvement in the battle showed his leadership and bravery but also contributed to the demoralization of his followers when they saw him injured.

And yet, at this critical point in the battle, the Muslim warriors rallied around their leader Muhammad (saw), who continued to give orders despite his injuries and encouraged his followers to fight on and withstand the Quraysh attacks. In the end, despite heavy losses, they managed to avert complete defeat. Muhammad (saw) and his remaining fighters were able to regroup on the Jabal Uhud hill. From there, they managed to fend off the Meccan attacks. The Quraysh, although successful on the battlefield, decided against a further attack, mainly because of the weakened state of their troops, the strategically better position of the Muslims, and the approaching evening. Abu Sufyan, the leader of the Quraysh, declared the battle over and withdrew with his troops back to Mecca.

Scarred by the defeat and the losses, including the Prophet's beloved uncle, Hamza (ra), the Muslims returned to Medina. The death of the Lion of Allah hit the Prophet very hard. It is narrated that Muhammad (saw) was deeply moved and saddened at the sight of his maimed uncle.

Hamza (ra) and many other dead Muslims were buried according to Islamic rites. This includes the ritual washing of the body, wrapping it in a simple cloth, and facing the body towards the Ka'ba in Mecca. The Prophet's uncle was henceforth regarded as a martyr whose courage and dedication to the cause of Islam were emphasized. The recounting of stories of his bravery and loyalty helped the Muslim community to place his death in a context of pride and hope, despite the immediate sadness of it.

Allah (swt) revealed Sura 5:32 (Al-Ma'idah - The Tablet):

Sura 5:32 (translated):
"[...] whoever kills a man without his having committed murder or without his having caused mischief on earth, it is as if he has killed all mankind; and whoever preserves the life of a man, it is as if he has preserved the life of all mankind. Our messengers came to them with clear proofs. However, many of them continued to transgress excessively on earth afterwards."

Inspired by this revelation of the Almighty, Muhammad (saw) changed the rules of warfare to prevent the repetition of acts of revenge such as the one against Hamza (ra). Muhammad (saw) thus issued specific ethical ground rules for warfare aimed at breaking the spiral of violence. He explicitly forbade the mutilation of the dead and demanded that the bodies of slain enemies be treated with respect. These new rules were intended to prevent cyclical acts of revenge leading to ever more bloodshed.

Furthermore, Muhammad (saw) emphasized the importance of existing Islamic teachings that preserve the dignity and rights of prisoners of war. He taught his followers that prisoners of war should be treated humanely, regardless of the actions of their leaders. This was in stark contrast to the prevailing practices of the time, in which prisoners of war were often severely mistreated. Equally new was that prisoners were now given adequate food rations and some who could read and write were given the opportunity to earn their freedom by teaching ten Muslim children. Through these changes, Muhammad (saw) not only established a more humane law of war within his community, but also laid the foundation for ethical warfare, which later became an integral part of Islamic law.

After the Battle of Uhud, the community in Medina first had to recover and regroup. The immediate impact was profound and emphasized the need to develop a stronger defense and a more robust military strategy. The Prophet Muhammad (saw) and his followers drew lessons from the mistakes of Uhud that led them to take a more cautious and organized approach in later conflicts.

The Campaign Against the Banu Mustaliq (The Battle of al-Muraysi')

At the beginning of the year 627, the Muslims under Muhammad (saw) were forced to lead a campaign against the Banu Mustaliq. The Banu Mustaliq were an influential Arab tribe found near the coastal region of Qudaid and traditionally allied with the Quraysh. (See 5. on Map 1) Due to their strategic location and abundant resources, as well as their potential threat to trade routes, relations between the Banu Mustaliq and the Muslims in Medina had been strained for some time. So, when the Prophet learned that the Banu Mustaliq under their leader Harith ibn Dirar were mobilizing troops, possibly in preparation for an attack, he decided to act first. Muhammad (saw) led a group of about 700 fighters into battle against the Banu Mustaliq. The Prophet had previously learned from a reliable source that many members of the Banu Mustaliq were staying at a water place called Muraisi. He went there with his fighters and cleverly exploited the element of surprise.

The attack was swift and effective; many members of the tribe were killed or captured. Among them was Juwayriya bint al-Harith, the daughter of the leader of the tribe, who was also captured. Juwayriya bint al-Harith later became one of the wives of the Prophet Muhammad (saw). Many of the captives were integrated into the Muslim community. The marriage of Muhammad (saw) to Juwayriya led to many Muslims freeing their slaves from the Banu Mustaliq tribe, which ensured peace between the two groups and strengthened Juwayriya's position within the community.

The Event of Slander ("Hadith al-Ifk")

But first, Muhammad (saw), his fighters, and the captives made their way back to Medina. It was customary for the Prophet to take one of his wives with him on his campaigns. In this case, it was Aisha (ra), the daughter of Abu Bakr (ra), whom he had already married in the year 620. When the caravan of Muslims stopped, Aisha (ra) left the camp briefly to relieve herself. When she wanted to return to the camp, she realized she had lost her necklace. She turned back to look for it. Meanwhile, Muhammad (saw) and the others moved on without her. It was mistakenly assumed that Aisha (ra) was still in her 'howdah' - a closed camel saddle in which the women traveled, and which offered protection from the scorching sun and desert sand. When Aisha (ra) returned, no one was there. She stayed behind alone and lay down in the sand, hoping that the others would soon notice her absence and pick her up.

Safwan ibn al-Mu'attal, an early member of the Muslim community in Medina, was known to follow the caravans at a distance, helping to collect items left behind or checking to see if they were being followed. And so, it was on this day. Safwan found Aisha (ra) sleeping in the sand the next morning. He recognized her and offered to help her. He got off his camel so that the wife of the Prophet Muhammad (saw) could ride on it.

When Safwan and Aisha (ra) finally caught up with the caravan, their arrival together caused quite a stir. The fact that Aisha (ra) was seen alone with a man (who was not one of her mahrams, i.e., men close to her by blood or marriage) immediately sparked the wildest rumors. Abdullah ibn Ubayy, a hypocrite and known opponent of the Prophet, who was one of the leaders of the city before the arrival of Muhammad (saw) in Medina, seized the opportunity to sow discord. He aimed to weaken the Prophet's position. So, he spread the rumor that more might have happened between Aisha (ra) and Safwan. This was a serious accusation. The rumor was actively spread by Abdullah ibn Ubayy and other munafiqun (hypocrites).

The Prophet found himself in a difficult situation as Aisha (ra) was his beloved wife and the accusations were taken very seriously by the community. He searched for ways to find out the truth and consulted various of his loyal companions for advice. Muhammad (saw) was emotionally affected by the incident and waited for a divine clarification on the matter. And the rumors did what they were supposed to: Tensions and divisions arose within the community.

Aisha (ra) knew nothing of the rumors until she returned to Medina. She noticed a change in her husband's attitude and others around her. Soon she learned of the outrageous rumors, which hurt her deeply. Aisha (ra) fell ill and withdrew to recover in peace.

Muhammad (saw) was not sure how to deal with the situation. After a month of uncertainty, he received a revelation from Allah (swt) during his afternoon rest, confirming Aisha's (ra) innocence and exposing the slander as lies.

These revelations can be found in the Holy Quran in Sura 24 (An-Nur - The Light). It was revealed that Aisha (ra) (and thus, of course, Safwan) was innocent.

Sura 24:11-13 (translated):
"Those who have spread the lie [about Aisha (ra)] are a group from among you. Do not think that it is bad for you; no, it is good for you. Each one of them is due the offense he has committed. And the one among them who had the major part in it shall receive a severe punishment."

Furthermore, the revelations of Allah (swt) demanded clear evidence for such accusations and at the same time severe punishments for those who were convicted of lying. The revelations also made it clear that in the case of accusations of fornication or adultery, four eyewitnesses who directly witnessed the act are required. This is stated in Sura 24:4 (An-Nur - The Light):

Sura 24:4 (translated):
"And those who accuse honorable women (without proof) and then do not produce four witnesses, strike them with eighty lashes and never accept testimony from them again. These are the true wrongdoers."

This high standard of proof was intended to ensure that such accusations would not be made lightly and served to protect people's privacy and honor.

After the revelation confirmed the innocence of Aisha (ra), Muhammad (saw) announced the punishment for the slanderers. The punishment was carried out publicly to show every Muslim the consequences of false accusations. All slanderers - including the wrongdoer Abdullah ibn Ubayy - were punished with 80 lashes, just as the Almighty had stipulated in his revelation.

Muhammad (saw) was then able to concentrate again on improving Medina's defense strategies. He forged alliances with surrounding Bedouin tribes, such as the Banu Asad, the Banu Ghifar, and the Banu Kinanah. In this way, the Prophet strengthened the defense of Medina's borders and secured the trade routes near Mecca, making the Muslims' caravans less vulnerable to Quraysh raids.

The Battle of the Trench

The Banu Nadir were one of the three major Jewish tribes in Medina and initially coexisted in peace with the Muslims. After the emigration of Muhammad (saw) to Medina, the Muslims and the Jewish tribes, including the Banu Nadir, concluded an alliance within the framework of the Document of Medina. This pact assured all allies of peaceful coexistence and mutual support and respect.

However, tensions between the Muslims and the Banu Nadir tribe in Medina gradually intensified. A decisive incident that ultimately led to the escalation was the murder of two men from the Banu Amir tribe. They had sought asylum with the Muslims in Medina because the Banu Nadir were persecuting them. Nevertheless, the two were killed by a member of the Banu Nadir.

However, the Banu Nadir refused to pay the blood money (diya) for the murder, which was a serious and unacceptable breach of contract. Muhammad (saw) decided to visit the Banu Nadir to discuss the matter of the blood money and to reach an agreement.

So, Muhammad (saw) set off with Abu Bakr (ra), Ali ibn Abi Talib (ra), and other companions to the fortress of the Banu Nadir. The Banu Nadir greeted Muhammad (saw) and his companions politely and agreed to discuss the compensation for the men who had been killed. Muhammad (saw) explained the importance of respecting the Treaty of Medina and emphasized the need to maintain peace and security in the city. The Banu Nadir listened and initially showed understanding. Then they withdrew to consult with each other.

While they were deliberating, the leaders of the Banu Nadir decided to kill Muhammad (saw). He had been a thorn in their side for some time, as they saw their political and economic influence threatened by the increasingly powerful Muslims. They hoped that the murder would decisively weaken the Muslims. At the time, the Prophet was sitting with his companions in front of one of the houses while waiting for the Banu Nadir leaders to return. They instructed a man to climb onto a roof and then drop a large stone on Muhammad (saw) to fatally injure him. But the cowardly plan failed. Muhammad (saw) received a divine revelation delivered to him by the angel Jibrīl, who warned him and revealed the sinister intentions of the Banu Nadir. Muhammad (saw) decided to break off the negotiations and leave the fortress without delay.

Thanks to the revelation of Allah (swt) and the quick reaction of the Prophet, they managed to escape.

After the attempted assassination of Muhammad (saw) became known, the Muslims regarded this as another serious breach of contract and a direct threat to the safety of their community. The Prophet and his companions decided to allow the Banu Nadir to leave Medina voluntarily. Muhammad (saw) wanted to avoid escalating the conflict and unnecessary bloodshed.

So, Muhammad (saw) sent his faithful follower Muhammad ibn Maslama to the Banu Nadir. He told them from the Prophet that they would be allowed to leave the city within ten days. They were also allowed to take all their movable goods with them. Particularly generous given the recent failed assassination attempt on Muhammad (saw), he also allowed the Banu Nadir to return once a year to bring in the harvest from their palm groves.

The Banu Nadir initially agreed, but shortly afterward, under the leadership of their tribal chief, decided to put up resistance in their fortresses within Medina. This led to a siege by the Muslims. They used various tactics to put pressure on the Banu Nadir. They cut off the supply routes into the fortress and eventually destroyed the palm groves around the fortress. The intention was to deprive the Banu Nadir of their economic basis and force them to give up.

During the siege, which lasted for around two weeks, there were minor skirmishes, and the treaty-breakers defended themselves by shooting arrows at the besiegers from the walls of their fortress. But despite the resistance, the living conditions in the fortress increasingly deteriorated - the tactics of Muhammad (saw) were a complete success. The Banu Nadir suffered from a lack of food and access to fresh water. After the siege, which lasted around two weeks, they were forced to surrender.

Muhammad (saw) allowed the Banu Nadir to leave the city and take what they could carry on 600 camels. This included their most valuable possessions. But now they were no longer given the opportunity to harvest their palm groves once a year. All their immovable possessions remained in Medina and were distributed among the Muslims, with a part being used for the needs of the community and to support the needy. Many Banu Nadir then moved to Khaybar, about 150 kilometers north of Medina, while others emigrated to Syria. However, the danger posed by the Banu Nadir was not yet completely averted...

While the Prophet was still taking precautions to protect Medina and safeguard the interests of the Muslims, a new alliance was formed in Mecca. The Banu Nadir were determined to take revenge on the Muslims in Medina and regain their properties and lands. Huyayy ibn Akhtab, a leader, traveled to Mecca to meet the Quraysh and negotiate a joint offensive against Medina. The Quraysh, who were only looking for a suitable opportunity to fight the Muslims, agreed. They wanted to crush the growing power of Muhammad (saw) and the Muslims once and for all.

With the help of the Banu Nadir, the Quraysh formed a coalition of various tribes, including the Banu Ghatafan and other Arab tribes. This united force became known as the "Ahzab" (confederation). Together they planned a large-scale offensive against Medina. In total, they mobilized a force of around 10,000 fighters, roughly three times the number of Quraysh troops at the Battle of Uhud.

Muhammad (saw) was aware of the threat posed by the coalition army. News of the forming alliance and its intentions reached him early on through spies and allies stationed outside Medina. The Muslims were therefore able to prepare for the impending large-scale attack. When Muhammad (saw) received the news of the army forming in Mecca, he immediately called his followers for a war council. Salman al-Farsi (ra) (the Persian), a loyal follower of the Prophet who had once come to Medina as a slave and then converted to Islam, had a good idea. He suggested digging a deep trench around the northeastern parts of Medina to neutralize the attackers' cavalry. The other flanks of Medina were already difficult for attackers to pass through due to the rocky terrain. The war council approved Salman's (ra) proposal and Muhammad (saw) ordered the Muslims to lend a hand given the impending attack. The Prophet took an active part in the excavation work, which motivated his followers. According to tradition, the construction of the trench took about six days.

The coalition army finally reached Medina at the end of March 627, but the attackers were surprised to find the moat, a defensive tactic they had not expected. They were unable to carry out their plan of a quick attack and instead had to set up camp some distance from the gates of Medina. They began the siege of the city, which was to last for around 27 days.

The attackers from Mecca were mainly experienced warriors and cavalrymen. They explored the length of the trench to find possible weak points. They looked for places where the trench was not so deep and wide or where natural features such as rocky outcrops or mounds of earth made it easier to cross. They also tried to fill up parts of the trench with earth and stones to create a passable path for the troops. This tactic was unsuccessful, however, as the attackers were exposed to direct archery and barrage fire from the Muslims during these actions. The best marksmen among the Muslims were able to kill many Meccans during the crossing attempts. The coalition army realized that all attempts to cross the rift would fail and looked for a way to weaken Medina from within. They aimed to undermine the alliances within Medina, especially the relations between the Muslims and the Banu Qurayza, a powerful Jewish tribe.

So, the Quraysh and their allies used envoys to enter secret negotiations with the Banu Qurayza. Huyayy ibn Akhtab, the leader of the Banu Nadir, played a key role in these negotiations. As a former resident of Medina, Huyayy knew the city and its surroundings very well and managed to enter the city unnoticed.

He went to Ka'b ibn Asad, the leader of the Banu Qurayza, to persuade him to break the alliance with Muhammad (saw). Initially, Ka'b ibn Asad hesitated, fearing the consequences of such a betrayal. After several meetings and under the pressure of the ongoing siege and Huyayy's assurances that the coalition army would surely win, Ka'b finally agreed to break the agreement with the Muslims.

However, the Muslims quickly became suspicious that something was wrong. It was noticed that the Banu Qurayza's behavior was changing. Muhammad (saw) sent spies to get to the bottom of this, as he was aware of the strategic importance of the alliance and wanted to be certain of the Banu Qurayza's betrayal.

Indeed, the Banu Qurayza made unusual military preparations and strengthened their fortresses within the city walls of Medina, which was interpreted as preparation for a possible attack against the Muslims. However, to remove all doubt, Muhammad (saw) decided to send a delegation to the Banu Qurayza. This delegation was to speak directly to the leader and clarify the rumors. According to reports, Ka'b received the delegation with hostility, openly confirming his breaking of the alliance with the Muslims. They now had two enemies - one standing outside the moat and besieging the city and an enemy within.

The Muslims had to react and strengthened their defensive lines within Medina, especially in the Muslim neighborhoods closest to the Banu Qurayza districts. The Prophet instructed reliable commanders to organize guards and ensure that all possible points of attack were secured. The reckoning with the treacherous Banu Qurayza was to take place after the Battle of the Trench.

Meanwhile, the Muslims had not remained idle and had infiltrated the besiegers, who had not succeeded in overcoming the moat, with spies. The task of the spies was to create mistrust among the besiegers. Particularly noteworthy is the role played by Nu'aym ibn Mas'ud, a former member of the Ghatafan tribe, who were part of the coalition against the Muslims. Secretly, Nu'aym had converted to Islam, and with Muhammad's (saw) approval, Nu'aym decided to sow discord among the attackers. He first went to the Banu Qurayza, with whom he had personal relations, and warned them not to trust the Quraysh. He claimed that if they failed in battle, the Quraysh would retreat and hand the Banu Qurayza over to the Muslims. After planting the seeds of distrust among the Banu Qurayza, Nu'aym went to the Quraysh and the Ghatafans and told them the Banu Qurayza had secretly made a truce with Muhammad (saw). He claimed that the Banu Qurayza were planning to hand over the Quraysh and Ghatafan leaders to the Muslims as a sign of their goodwill.

This clever list and the rumors spread led to considerable tension among the besiegers. The Quraysh and their allies began to question the loyalty of the Banu Qurayza, and, conversely, the Banu Qurayza became suspicious of the Quraysh's intentions. These growing uncertainties paralyzed the besiegers' ability to act and undermined their willingness to take coordinated action that could have endangered the Muslims.

The plan of Muhammad (saw) and Nu'aym ibn Mas'ud worked: a determined offensive by the coalition forces against Medina from outside and within was averted. The Muslim inhabitants of Medina could also rely on the support of Allah (swt).

He caused strong winds to blow up and the attackers' camp to be battered by violent sandstorms. The wind was so strong that it knocked over tents, extinguished fires, and caused panic among the attackers. Given the severely deteriorating weather, the Quraysh and the Ghatafan decided to retreat. After the battle, Sura 33:25 (Al-Ahzab - The Allies) was revealed to Muhammad (saw):

There were very few deaths among the Muslims, thanks to the sophisticated defense strategy and divine support.

The Siege of the Fortresses of the Treacherous Banu Qurayza

After the threat from the Quraysh and their allies had been repelled by the successful defense in the Battle of the Trench, Muhammad (saw) and the Muslims turned their attention to internal treachery.

The Prophet ordered the siege of the Banu Qurayza fortresses, which lasted about three weeks in total. The Muslims proceeded tactically, cutting off the traitors from supplies of food, water, and other necessary resources. The prospect of a prolonged siege with no hope of external support or successful defense made the Banu Qurayza's situation hopeless. Faced with this situation, the Banu Qurayza finally chose to surrender. They did so on the condition that their fate would be decided by the judgment of one of their former allies from the tribe of Aws, Sa'd ibn Mu'adh. Sa'd was the leader of the Aws and had converted to Islam shortly after the arrival of Muhammad (saw) and his followers in Medina. He had already fought in the battles of Badr and Uhud and had been seriously wounded by an arrow in the Battle of the Trench. The Banu Qurayza hoped for a lenient sentence from their former ally, who had kept close relations with them before he was wounded in battle.

However, the sentence that Sa'd passed was harsh. He ordered the execution of the able-bodied male members of the Banu Qurayza and the enslavement of the women and children. This reflected the severity of the treason they had committed against the Muslims. The sentence was based on the Jewish laws in force at the time, which stipulated the death penalty for treason. Historical estimates of the number of men executed vary, with figures ranging from 400 to 900. The executions took place in Medina, where the men were beheaded. Shortly after the sentence was pronounced, Sa'd ibn Mu'adh succumbed to his severe injuries.

The successful defense of Medina against the coalition army from Mecca and the decisive handling of the treachery of the Banu Qurayza greatly strengthened the authority of the Prophet Muhammad (saw). His leadership role was confirmed, and his strategic decisions during and after the conflicts were widely regarded as justified by the Muslim population. All this cemented the Prophet's status as the political and spiritual leader of the Muslim community. And so, Muhammad (saw) worked to strengthen the concept of the Ummah, a joined community that transcended traditional tribal ties and encompassed all Muslims. He emphasized religious and social equality and brotherhood among Muslims, regardless of their ethnic or social background. In this way, Muhammad (saw) succeeded in creating a strong sense of belonging and loyalty that went far beyond previously existing tribal loyalties.

"Be ye therefore steadfast. Verily, the promise of Allah is true. And those who are not convinced should not cause you to waver."

(Ar-Rum 30:60)

Please pause.

Ibrahim Al-Abadi and Path of Islam are convinced that Muslims must always remain united and strong to spread Islam together. So if you like this book, feel free to recommend it to your family, friends and relatives. Even non-Muslims can learn about Islam and find the path to Allah with the help of this book.

If you like this book, please support us by leaving an honest review.

You can rate the book using the following link or QR code:

Have you found any errors? Of course, we are open to your criticism and welcome your suggestions so that we can further develop this work to the greater satisfaction of Allah 羰.

Feel free to email us at **info@islamway-books.com**

Shkran!

Ibrahim Al-Abadi & Islam Way

Chapter

6

Campaigns and Key Events in the Late Life of Muhammad (saw)

The Treaty of Hudaybiyya

After the Battle of the Trench and the subsequent expulsion of the Banu Qurayza, there was a period of relative calm in Medina. The Prophet Muhammad (saw) used this time to further strengthen the still-young community and to establish diplomatic relations with other tribes and rulers. A significant event in the year 628 was a short pilgrimage (Umrah) to Mecca, which Muhammad (saw) had decided to undertake. Of course, this was not without danger, as the Quraysh, the archenemies of the Muslims, controlled Mecca.

But Muhammad (saw) was full of hope and confidence. Moreover, the Prophet wanted to demonstrate both the peacefulness of Islam and to assert the right of Muslims to go on pilgrimage. He was not afraid of the Quraysh.

Muhammad (saw) set off for Mecca with around 1,400 of his companions. They wore pilgrim robes (ihram) and were unarmed to emphasize their peaceful intentions. The Muslims also brought sacrificial animals with them.

When the Muslims finally reached the town of Hudaybiyya near Mecca, the Quraysh learned of their arrival. They decided to deny them access to the city. The Muslims then set up camp on the spot to wait and discuss how to continue.

The Quraysh first sent a scout named Budayl ibn Warqa from the Khuza'a tribe to investigate the situation and gather information about the Muslims. Budayl recognized the peaceful intentions of the Muslims and reported this to the Quraysh. Although the Muslims were unarmed and thus an easy target, the Quraysh decided not to confront Muhammad (saw) and the Muslims at Hudaybiyya by force for several reasons. The Muslims had come in pilgrims' garb, which was a clear sign of peaceful intentions. Attacking pilgrims was considered a serious breach of tradition and decency, even in pre-Islamic Arab culture. This would have severely damaged the reputation of the Quraysh throughout the Arabian Peninsula. Furthermore, the Muslims were now a well-organized and increasingly strong community. The Quraysh knew that an attack could potentially lead to major conflicts that might not end well for them either.

So, the Quraysh decided to send representatives to the Muslims to clarify the situation. Mikraz ibn Hafs was one of the first messengers. However, his visit did not bring any decisive progress but showed that the Quraysh were prepared to negotiate. The Meccans then sent Urwa ibn Mas'ud, a well-known and respected Quraysh leader. He was to continue the negotiations with the Muslim pilgrims. He appeared before Muhammad (saw) and began to explain why the Muslims should return to Medina without continuing the pilgrimage. But Muhammad (saw) remained steadfast and calm. He explained to Urwa that they had not come to fight, but to peacefully perform the Umra, the lesser pilgrimage. The Prophet emphasized their determination, even if they had to put themselves in danger to do so.

During the conversation, Urwa observed the behavior of the Prophet's companions. He was impressed by the loyalty and devotion of the Muslims towards Muhammad (saw). A notable moment was when Abu Bakr (ra) harshly rejected Urwa when he spoke disrespectfully to the Prophet. This showed Urwa the determination and deep respect that the Muslims had for their leader. After the conversation, Urwa returned to the Quraysh and reported on his impressions. He described the discipline and devotion of the Muslims and recommended that the Quraysh accommodate the Muslims and seek a peaceful path. Urwa told the Quraysh that he had visited many kingdoms but had never seen a group of followers who revered their leader as much as the Muslims revered Muhammad (saw). Although no agreement had yet been reached, the Quraysh became aware of the Muslims' determination and peaceful intentions.

Then the Quraysh sent the next messenger, Hulays ibn Alqamah. Hulays was the leader of the Ahabish, a group of tribes allied with the Quraysh. He was impressed by the honesty and peacefulness of the Muslims. He saw that they had brought offerings for the pilgrimage and was also certain that they had no warlike intentions. On his return, he said that the Muslims were honest pilgrims and that he supported them in their endeavor. However, when the Quraysh still did not allow the Muslims to enter Mecca, Muhammad (saw) decided to send a messenger to the Meccans himself. His choice fell on Uthman ibn Affan (ra). Uthman (ra) was a loyal follower of the Prophet and a respected man among the Quraysh. Muhammad (saw) hoped that this would facilitate the negotiations and open the gates of Mecca for them.

Uthman (ra) stayed in Mecca for several days. During his stay, he tried to convince the Quraysh to finally grant the Muslims access to the Ka`ba so that they could complete their pilgrimage. However, the Quraysh still refused to give in and rejected his proposals. There are varying accounts of Uthman's treatment during his stay. Some traditions suggest that Uthman (ra) was held hostage to exert pressure on the Muslims. This led to a rumor among the Muslims that Uthman (ra) had been killed. This in turn increased tensions and led to the so-called "oath of allegiance under the tree" (Bay'at al-Ridwan).

Muhammad (saw) called the Muslims together under a large tree and informed them of the rumors about Uthman's fate. He called on the Muslims to swear allegiance to him. His followers did not hesitate for a moment and placed their hands on the Prophet's hand one after the other and swore allegiance to him. They vowed to sacrifice their lives if necessary to defend the Prophet and Islam. Since Uthman (ra) was not present, Muhammad (saw) symbolically placed his left hand on his right hand and declared this as Uthman's oath of allegiance.

Later, Muhammad (saw) said about the Muslims who had sworn allegiance to him under the tree:

[...] *"None of those who took the oath of allegiance under the tree will enter the fire."*
Jami` at-Tirmidhi, Book 49, Hadith 3860

But shortly afterward, something surprising happened. Uthman (ra) returned unharmed to the Muslims in Hudaybiyya after the negotiations in Mecca had failed.

Shortly after Uthman's arrival, he was followed by Suhayl ibn Amr, another Quraysh negotiator, who continued the negotiations with Muhammad (saw). Suhayl emphasized the need to keep peace and to postpone the Muslim pilgrimage until the following year. This was very important to the Quraysh.

They wanted to avoid a possible confrontation in Mecca at all costs. The Muslims were many and although they had peaceful intentions, the Meccans feared that their sudden arrival in Mecca could lead to tension and possibly even violence.

Eventually, Muhammad (saw) and Suhayl came to an agreement and recorded it in the Treaty of Hudaybiyya:

Ten-year ceasefire: Both parties agreed not to take hostile action against each other for ten years. This agreement was intended to ensure long-term peace in the region.

Return of Muslims to Medina: Muslims should not go on pilgrimage to Mecca this year but return to Medina.

Pilgrimage the following year: Muslims were allowed to return to Mecca the following year (629) to perform a three-day pilgrimage.

No weapons except travel swords: When Muslims go on pilgrimage to Mecca the following year, they are not allowed to carry any weapons with them, except for their traveling swords, which should always remain in their sheaths.

Obligation to extradite defectors: If a Quraysh defected to the Muslims in Medina, he had to be brought back to Mecca. Conversely, however, no Muslims who defected to the Quraysh had to be extradited.

Free choice of alliance: The Arab tribes were free to decide whether they wanted to join the Muslims or the Quraysh without fear of reprisals from the other side.

Many of the Muslims were disappointed and frustrated, as they wanted to start the pilgrimage immediately and saw the treaty as advantageous, especially for the Quraysh. They had prepared for it and were eager to visit the holy sites immediately. The decision to wait a year was difficult for them to accept. But Muhammad (saw) reassured his followers. He emphasized that the Treaty of Hudaybiyya was a significant step towards peace, showed a strong faith in Allah's (swt) plan, and emphasized that the treaty was ultimately for the benefit of the Muslims. He encouraged his companions to trust Allah (swt) and recognize the wisdom behind the postponement of the pilgrimage.

To reaffirm the treaty and to reassure the Muslims, he had them sacrifice the sacrificial animals on the spot and cut their hair, which were normally rituals of the pilgrimage. These symbolic acts helped the Muslims maintain the spirit of the pilgrimage and accept the treaty.

During this time of disappointment, Allah (swt) revealed an important message to the Prophet Muhammad (saw), which is recorded in Sura 48:1 (al-Fath - Victory):

> **Sura 48:1 (translated):**
> **"Certainly, We have given you a clear victory."**

This revelation confirmed that the Treaty of Hudaybiyya was a clear victory for the Muslims. The treaty meant that the Muslims, and thus the Ummah of the Prophet Muhammad (saw), were officially recognized by the Quraysh.

The Battle of Khaybar

Shortly after the Treaty of Hudaybiyya, the Prophet Muhammad (saw) decided to conquer Khaybar. After the expulsion of the Banu Nadir from Medina, many of them had settled there. Together with other Jewish tribes, they continued their efforts to fight the Muslims. It was therefore not a breach of the Treaty of Hudaybiyya, as the tribes living there posed a threat to the Muslims.

Muhammad (saw) prepared his troops and marched to Khaybar in March 628 with around 1,600 fighters. Under the leadership of the Prophet, the Muslims planned the route carefully so that the element of surprise was on their side, and they could minimize the losses in their ranks.

Khaybar consisted of several fortified strongholds strategically distributed on hills. These fortresses were well-defended and difficult to conquer. The siege began with a targeted offensive against the weaker fortresses. The first fortress to be targeted was an-Natāt. The siege lasted for several days. After intense fighting and sustained pressure, the defenders finally surrendered, and the fortress fell into Muslim hands. After the success at an-Natāt, Muhammad (saw) and his forces turned to the fortress of as-Sa'b ibn Mu'adh, which was more heavily fortified. Fierce battles ensued in which both sides suffered heavy losses. However, after a series of intense attacks and strategic maneuvers, the Muslims were finally able to take this fortress as well.

The al-Qamus fortress was the most important and most heavily fortified in Khaybar. This made it a central target for the Muslim forces. The siege began with cutting off supplies and constant attacks. When this was unsuccessful, Muhammad (saw) chose Ali ibn Abi Talib (ra) to take the lead in further attacks. Ali (ra) was an excellent fighter and known for his bravery. With a group of his best warriors, he approached the fortress with great caution. He then stepped in front of the main gate of the fortress and challenged the defenders to an open battle.

Marhab, one of the strongest warriors in Khaybar, accepted the challenge. He stepped in front of the gate with a small group of defenders. A duel ensued between Ali (ra) and Marhab. At the same time, Ali's companions fought against the troop that had accompanied Marhab. It was an epic battle in which Ali (ra) finally succeeded in killing his opponent. Marhab's companions also fell in battle against the brave Muslims.

After the loss of their strongest warrior, the remaining defenders in the fortress were demoralized. Shortly afterward, the Muslim fighters succeeded in conquering the fortress with an intensified attack. The remaining Jewish tribes in Khaybar, who had previously put up fierce resistance, finally capitulated. They asked for negotiations to save their lives and some of their possessions.

In his infinite kindness, the Prophet accepted the surrender - under certain conditions.

The Prophet Muhammad (saw) decided that the conquered land and goods of Khaybar should be considered "Ghanimah" (spoils of war). This meant that the land was distributed among the Muslims, with a part reserved for the community and the wealth of the Ummah (Muslim community). Thus, the inhabitants of Khaybar had to give up their fortresses and weapons but were allowed to continue living on the land and cultivating it. In return, they were to give half of their earnings to the Muslims as a tax (kharaj).

After the conquest of Khaybar, Safiyya bint Huyayy (ra), the daughter of one of the leaders of the Banu Nadir, was captured. Shortly afterward, she embraced Islam and later became the wife of Muhammad (saw), which contributed to the further integration of the conquered peoples.

The Muslim Expeditions and the Battle of Mu'ta

After the Treaty of Hudaybiyya was concluded and after the victory in the Battle of Khaybar, Muhammad (saw) used the peace with the Quraysh to further spread Islam and strengthen the diplomatic relations of Muslims with other peoples. The Prophet wanted to carry the message of Allah (swt) beyond the borders of the Arabian Peninsula and thus ensure the international recognition of Islam. So, he sent letters to various rulers and heads of state, including Heraclius, the emperor of Byzantium, and Khosrau II, the king of the Sassanid Empire. The letters were delivered by his closest companions and always began with the sentence, "In the name of Allah, the All-Merciful, the Merciful." The rulers were called upon to accept Islam and follow the teachings of the Prophet.

This is the letter that Muhammad (saw) sent to Khosrau II, the king of the Sassanid Empire:

In the name of Allah, the All-Merciful.

From Muhammad, the servant and messenger of Allah, to the great ruler of Persia, Khosrau.

Peace be upon him who follows guidance.

I hereby invite you to Islam. Accept Islam and you will be in peace and security and Allah will double your reward.

> *However, if you turn away from the message of Allah, the sins of all your subjects will also fall on you. I urge you to consider the following:*
>
> *"O People of the Book! Come to a word that is equal between us and you, that we worship none but Allah and associate nothing with Him, and that some of us do not lord it over others except Allah. But if they turn away, then say, 'Bear witness that we are devoted to Allah.*
>
> *Muhammad, the Messenger of Allah*

The wording of the other letters hardly differed. Nevertheless, the reactions of the rulers were very different. Heraclius, the emperor of Byzantium, showed interest in the message of Allah (swt) and did some research. However, he did not convert to Islam. Khosrau II reacted angrily to the letter of Muhammad (saw), tore it up, and ordered the messenger to be arrested. When the Prophet learned of this reaction, he said: "May Allah also tear up his kingdom." This prophecy later came true with the Muslim conquests of the Sassanid Empire under the Rashidun caliphs.

Negus of Abyssinia showed respect and kindness towards the letter and assessed the Prophet's message as positive. Nevertheless, there was no clear sign that he had officially converted to Islam. The Muqawqis, ruler of Egypt, responded politely and sent gifts to the Prophet, including two female slaves, one of whom, Mary al-Qibtiyya, later became a wife of the Prophet and bore him a son named Ibrâhîm.

Although none of the rulers officially embraced Islam, the letters nevertheless positively impacted and helped to establish Islam as a significant political and religious force. The polite responses of most rulers, especially the Negus of Abyssinia and the Muqawqis of Egypt, helped to avoid hostilities and facilitated peaceful relations. Furthermore, word of the interactions with the Muslims spread and had a positive influence on the inhabitants, as many people in the respective regions converted to Islam over time.

However, the king of the Sassanid Empire did not want to simply accept this letter, which he saw as presumptuous. So Khosrau II decided to act against the Prophet. He ordered Badhan, the governor of Yemen, to take Muhammad (saw) prisoner. Shortly afterward two men were sent to Medina to carry out this order.

When the men arrived in Medina, they immediately sought out Muhammad (saw). They gave him the news of Badhan and the order from Khosrau II to take him prisoner. The atmosphere was tense because the men were aware of the possible consequences of their mission. But Muhammad (saw) received the men and calmly listened to their message. The men explained that they had come on behalf of Khosrau II to arrest him and bring him to Persia. The Prophet Muhammad (saw) nevertheless remained calm and spoke kindly to the men. He explained to them that Allah (swt) had revealed to him that Khosrau II would be murdered by his son. He told them to return to Badhan to tell him this news. The men were astonished by these words and at the same time impressed by the Prophet's self-assurance. They made their way back to Yemen. There they told Badhan what the Prophet Muhammad (saw) had said. Badhan was skeptical at first. But shortly afterward the news reached him that Chosrau II had indeed been murdered by his son and that the prophecy of Muhammad (saw) had thus been fulfilled. Impressed by the wisdom of the

Prophet, Badhan embraced Islam. Many of his followers also converted to Islam, and control of Yemen passed peacefully to the Muslims.

The Prophet's messengers, who continued to distribute Muhammad's (saw) letters to the rulers, were not always received kindly. When Muhammad (saw) sent an envoy to the ruler of Busra, a region in the Byzantine Empire, he was killed by a Ghassanid tribal leader. This was not only a serious breach of diplomatic immunity, but a provocation against the Muslims that forced Muhammad (saw) to respond militarily.

So, he raised an army of 3,000 men to act against the Ghassanids. This was one of the largest armies the Muslims had raised at that time. Muhammad (saw) appointed Zayd ibn Haritha as the leader of the expedition. If Zayd was killed, Jafar ibn Abi Talib and then Abdullah ibn Rawaha were to take command. Muhammad (saw) remained in Medina to take care of the daily affairs.

The Muslim army marched north towards Mu'ta, a place near the present-day city of Karak in Jordan. (See 6. on map 1) When the Muslim army arrived there, it turned out that the Byzantine forces and their Arab allies had assembled a massive army. Reports on troop numbers vary widely, ranging from 10,000 to 100,000 soldiers.

The battle began. It was a veritable slaughter. Zayd ibn Haritha bravely led the Muslim army but was killed in battle. Jafar ibn Abi Talib then took command and fought bravely until he too was killed. Abdullah ibn Rawaha then took command and was also killed by his enemies. After the death of the three leaders, Khalid ibn al-Walid took command. Khalid, who later received the honorary title "Sword of Allah", had emigrated to Medina after the Treaty of Hudaybiyya and converted to Islam. The former enemy of Muhammad (saw)

was able to avert the catastrophe and ordered the Muslim retreat. Thus, he could return the survivors to Medina in an orderly fashion.

Although the Muslims were greatly outnumbered and suffered heavy losses, Khalid ibn al-Walid managed to save the army from complete annihilation. The retreat was regarded as a tactical masterstroke, and Khalid's leadership qualities were greatly appreciated by the Muslims. After the army returned to Medina, Muhammad (saw) praised the bravery of the fighters and especially Khalid ibn al-Walid for his tactical skill.

The Short Pilgrimage (Umrah) to Mecca

In the year 629 (7th year after the Hijrah), the Muslims under the leadership of the Prophet Muhammad (saw) prepared to travel to Mecca to perform the minor pilgrimage known as the Umrah al-Qada. This was done according to the terms of the Treaty of Hudaybiyya, which allowed Muslims to perform the pilgrimage the following year.

Around 2,000 Muslims joined the Prophet Muhammad (saw) on the journey to Mecca. They all donned the pilgrim's garb (ihram) to show their peaceful intentions and perform the rituals of Umrah. When they finally reached Mecca, they entered the city peacefully. The Quraysh had withdrawn from Mecca for three days to give the Muslims the space and peace to perform their religious rituals undisturbed.

The Muslims performed tawaf at the Ka'ba under the guidance of the Prophet. Muhammad (saw) went to the corner of the Ka`ba where the black stone (Hajar al-Aswad) was embedded. Then the Prophet kissed the black stone and circled the Ka`ba seven times in a clockwise direction. Each time he passed the black stone, Muhammad (saw) kissed it again. His followers did the same as the Prophet. They then walked back and forth seven times between the hills of Safa and Marwah (Sa'i). This still reminds us of Hagar, the wife of the Prophet Ibrâhîm (as), who searched between these hills for water for her son Isma'il (as) and where the spring Zamzam opened. At the end of the Umrah, the men cut or shortened their hair. The women cut out a small strand of hair. This symbolizes spiritual purification.

The Quraysh had adhered to the Treaty of Hudaybiyya and the Umrah proceeded without incident or bloodshed.

The Conquest of Mecca

However, the Treaty of Hudaybiyya did not last long. There had long been a feud between the Banu Bakr, an allied tribe of the Quraysh, and the Banu Khuza'a, who were allied with the Muslims, which the Treaty of Hudaybiyya had temporarily settled.

The Banu Bakr decided to break the peace and attack the Banu Khuza'a. They were secretly supported by the Quraysh, who provided them with weapons. The Banu Khuza'a had not expected an attack and were taken by surprise. The surviving members of the Banu Khuza'a fled to Medina to seek protection from the Muslims. They asked the Prophet Muhammad (saw) for help and told him about the Banu Bakr's breach of contract and the involvement of the Quraysh. The Prophet saw the raid as a clear breach of the Treaty of Hudaybiyya and a direct threat to the security of the Muslim community. He decided to take military action against the Quraysh and formed an army. With around 10,000 men, the Muslims marched to Mecca in January 630.

When they reached Marr al-Zahran, just a few kilometers from Mecca, Muhammad (saw) instructed his followers to light more bonfires than necessary to make the force look even larger. The Quraysh were overwhelmed by the superiority of the Muslim army. The Meccans were aware they were militarily inferior and would hardly survive an open confrontation against the well-equipped Muslim army. Abu Sufyan, one of the leading heads of the Quraysh, came to the Muslim camp to negotiate. Abu Sufyan was accompanied by Muhammad's (saw) uncle, Abbas ibn Abdul Muttalib, who met him by chance and helped him get safely to the Muslim camp.

Abu Sufyan explained to the Prophet that he had come to find a peaceful solution and save the city from possible destruction. He was deeply impressed by the discipline of the Muslim troops, realized that the Quraysh had no chance militarily, and was looking for a way to surrender.

Muhammad (saw) showed a willingness to negotiate but set clear conditions for the surrender of Mecca. He demanded that the Quraysh submit to Muslim rule. Abu Sufyan hesitated at first. But after long talks and given the military superiority of the Muslims, he agreed. He also declared his willingness to accept Islam. He made the profession of faith (Shahada) and converted. This was a strategic move by Abu Sufyan to secure his position within the new order.

The Prophet then told Abu Sufyan that no harm would come to the people of Mecca as long as they did not rise against the Muslims or show hostility. Moreover, anyone who stayed in his house and locked the door would be safe. The same applied to the house of Abu Sufyan and the Ka'ba. Thus, there were various places of refuge for the inhabitants of Mecca.

After the negotiations, Abu Sufyan returned to Mecca to calm the inhabitants and explain the terms of surrender to them. Shortly afterward, the Muslims marched peacefully into the city under the leadership of the Prophet. The army had split up and poured into the city from all directions through the gates of Mecca. Most inhabitants remained in their homes or sought refuge in the safe houses and the Ka`ba - as was imposed on them as part of the conditions.

Resistance was only sporadic and was quickly quelled. The Muslims showed great restraint and refrained from violence, which led to the almost peaceful takeover of the city. Muhammad (saw) once again proved his infinite wisdom, mercy, and strategic foresight by taking the city without unnecessary bloodshed and protecting the inhabitants from reprisals.

After the peaceful surrender of Mecca, Muhammad (saw) immediately went to the Ka`ba, accompanied by some of his closest companions, including Ali ibn Abi Talib (ra). As he entered the Ka`ba, he recited the takbir ("Allahu Akbar", which means "Allah is the greatest") to emphasize the omnipotence of Allah (swt). In the Ka`ba and around the building there were still idols and statues worshipped by the Quraysh and other pagan tribes. The Prophet Muhammad (saw) began to knock the idols to the ground and destroy them. As he did so, he recited Sura 17:81 (Al-Isra - The Night Journey):

Sura 17:81 (translated):
"And say: The truth has come, and the false has vanished.
Verily, the false is always a vanishing thing."

After the destruction of the idols, the Prophet had the Ka'ba cleansed. This included the removal of all symbols and relics of polytheism that were found in the Ka`ba ba and its surroundings. When the cleaning was completed, Muhammad (saw) prayed two rak'ah (units of prayer) to dedicate the Ka`ba to Allah (swt) as a sacred place of worship. Immediately after the Prophet's prayer, Bilal ibn Rabah (ra) ascended to the roof of the Ka`ba and called out the Adhan (call to prayer). Thus, he proclaimed the new spiritual order of Mecca.

As agreed as part of the terms of Mecca's surrender, Muhammad (saw) declared an amnesty for the Quraysh and all other inhabitants of Mecca. This included many former enemies of Islam. Many inhabitants of Mecca were very impressed by the Prophet's mercy and character and embraced Islam.

To restore order in the city, Muhammad (saw) assigned various administrative positions. Khalid ibn al-Walid was entrusted with the responsibility of ensuring the military security of the city. The Prophet (saw) appointed Bilal ibn Rabah (ra) to issue the call to prayer (adhan). His appointment had great symbolic significance, as Bilal (ra) was one of the Prophet's first and most loyal companions and a former slave who was freed by Islam.

Gradually, the laws of Islam were introduced, and the legal system was restructured based on Sharia law. The earlier traditional structures in Mecca were largely retained as long as they complied with Islamic principles. Muhammad (saw) addressed the inhabitants of Mecca in several public speeches. He explained the new guidelines and commandments to them and always emphasized unity and brotherhood among Muslims, regardless of their tribal affiliation or earlier conflicts. He introduced reforms aimed at ensuring social and economic justice, including the elimination of usury (riba).

The Prophet Muhammad (saw) emphasized the importance of Hajj (major pilgrimage) and Umrah (minor pilgrimage) as central religious practices of Muslims. These rituals should now be performed according to Islamic regulations.

One year after the peaceful capture of Mecca, Muhammad (saw) received a revelation from Allah (swt). Sura 9:28 (At-Tawbah - Repentance) forbade non-Muslims to enter Mecca and the Ka'ba (Holy Mosque).

Sura 9:28 (translated):
"O you who believe that the idolaters are indeed impure, do not let them approach the Sacred Mosque after this year of theirs. And if you fear poverty, Allah will make you rich from His bounty if He wills. Indeed, Allah is All-Knowing, All-Wise."

So, the Prophet declared Mecca and the Ka'bah holy places of Islam, which only Muslims were allowed to enter. For many years, the pilgrimages of idol worshippers to the Ka'ba had meant considerable income for the inhabitants of Mecca. However, the Sura At-Tawbah - Repentance reassured the believers that Allah (swt) would provide for them from His bounty and that they need not fear economic hardship.

The Battle of Hunayn and the Campaign to Taif

After the conquest of Mecca, Muhammad (saw) began to consolidate the power of Islam in the region. He made alliances with Arab tribes who lived near the city. However, some, especially the Hawazin and Thaqif tribes, felt increasingly threatened by the growing power of the Muslims. They therefore decided to form an alliance and rise against Islam. They wanted to defend their independence and traditional beliefs at all costs and planned an attack.

News of the impending Hawazin and Thaqif offensive reached Muhammad (saw), who reacted immediately and raised an army of around 12,000 fighters. Among them were many of the new converts from Mecca as well as the Muslims from Medina. Led by the Prophet himself, the Muslim troops marched towards Hunayn, a valley between Mecca and Taif, where the enemy tribes had gathered. (See 4. on map 2)

The Battle of Hunayn began on January 10, 630, when the troops of Muhammad (saw) were surprised by the well-prepared and hidden troops of Hawazin and Thaqif as they advanced through the valley of Hunayn. The enemies of Islam had prepared an ambush and ambushed the Prophet's troops. This caused disorder and panic, which led to a chaotic retreat. Many Muslims fled the battlefield. However, the Prophet Muhammad (saw) remained steadfast and called on his companions to return and attack again. With his courage and determination, he managed to rally the fighters and lead them to a counterattack. His troops finally gained the upper hand and were able to put the enemy to flight. The strategic use of bows and arrows, and cavalry, played an important role in the Muslims' victory. However, the Prophet's army also received divine support. Allah (swt) sent angels to help them, who were instrumental in defeating the enemy forces.

Later, Sura 9:25-26 (At-Tawbah - Repentance) was revealed to the Prophet.

Sura 9:25-26 (translated):
"Indeed, Allah has already helped you to victory in many places and on the day of Hunayn, when your great numbers made you overconfident, but you were of no use. The earth became narrow for you despite its vastness,

After the victory, the Muslims took a large number of spoils of war, including weapons, livestock, and prisoners. Among them were many women and children of the Hawazin. The victory strengthened the military and political power of Islam in the region. Many defeated tribes accepted the new religion and became part of the Muslim community.

Shortly after the battle, a delegation of the defeated tribes came to the Prophet Muhammad (saw) and asked for the release of their families. The Prophet showed generosity and released most of the captives.

After the Battle of Hunayn, the Prophet Muhammad (saw) led his troops to Taif to besiege the city of the Thaqif. This siege lasted for several weeks but was ultimately unsuccessful. Muhammad (saw) decided to withdraw his troops and march to Mecca.

The Return to Medina

Back in Mecca, Muhammad (saw) distributed the spoils of war from the Battle of Hunayn. The Prophet ensured a fair distribution of this booty among the Muslims and the new converts. He then set off on the journey back to Medina with some of his closest companions. Some new converts from Mecca and other areas joined the Prophet to receive further instruction in Islam.

In the same year, the Thaqif sent a delegation to Medina to negotiate peace terms with the Prophet Muhammad (saw). An important part of the negotiations was the question of the idols in Taif. The Thaqif asked for a grace period to destroy the idols and fully embrace Islam. The Prophet Muhammad (saw) granted this request and accepted the conditions to ease the transition to Islam. After this period, the tribe finally accepted Islam and submitted to Muslim rule. Thus, the conflict was settled peacefully.

The Campaign to Tabuk

At the end of the year 630, the next threat was to challenge the Muslim community.

There were rumors that the Byzantine Empire was raising a large army to attack Medina. These rumors worried the Prophet and necessitated a quick response. Instead of waiting for a possible attack by the Byzantines, Muhammad (saw) decided to take the initiative and tackle the threat directly. This was not only to protect the Muslims but also to show their strength and determination.

Tabuk is in the northwest of the Arabian Peninsula, about 700 kilometers from Medina. (See 7. on map 1) This region was of strategic importance for several reasons. Important trade routes leading from Mecca via Medina to Syria ran through Tabuk. Control over Tabuk meant control over these trade routes. Tabuk was also an ideal starting point for a possible invasion from the north. The Byzantines could have used this region as a base from which to launch attacks on Muslim territories.

Muhammad (saw) called on the Muslims to follow him to Tabuk. He emphasized the need to face the threat of the Byzantines. Many responded to his call, but others were afraid of the Byzantine army and the region was afflicted by rather hot weather, which would make the campaign very difficult.

Nevertheless, the Prophet raised an army of around 30,000 soldiers, the largest Muslim force at the time. As sufficient provisions and equipment had to be carried for the long journey to Tabuk, the campaign posed a significant logistical challenge. Thanks to wealthy Muslims such as Abu Bakr, some of whom equipped the soldiers out of their own pockets, this number of troops could be achieved.

The march to Tabuk was long and arduous, as the route led through the scorching hot desert. Nevertheless, the Muslim army showed great determination and discipline.

During the expedition through the hot desert sands, Muhammad (saw) received a revelation from Allah (swt), which is recorded in the Holy Quran in Sura 9:81-82 (At-Tawbah - Repentance) and condemns those who did not join the campaign to Tabuk.

Sura 9:81-82 (translated):
"Those who have been left behind rejoice that they have remained at home, unlike the Messenger of God. It is repugnant to them to wage war with their wealth and in their own persons for the sake of God, and they say: 'Do not go out in the heat!' Say: 'The fire of hell is hotter. If only they would accept reason! They will have only a short time to laugh, but a long time to weep, as a reward for what they have committed.'"

After arriving in Tabuk, the Muslim army set up a camp. However, they found no Byzantine army there. It turned out that the Byzantines had either changed their plans, or the reports of their invasion might have been false.

In his great wisdom, Muhammad (saw) used his stay in Tabuk to negotiate with local tribes. The Prophet concluded peace treaties and alliances with many of these tribes. This played a decisive role in strengthening the position of the Muslims in the region and securing their northern borders.

Although there was no direct military conflict with the Byzantines, the expedition to Tabuk was nevertheless a success, as it proved the strength of the Muslim army, and new alliances were formed. After about 20 days in Tabuk, Muhammad (saw) decided to return to Medina. The journey back was also arduous, but the army returned safely.

Chapter

7

The Farewell Pilgrimage ("Hajj al-Wada")

In the tenth year after the Hijrah (in 632), the Prophet Muhammad (saw) announced that he would perform the Hajj. Word spread quickly and thousands of Muslims from all over the Arabian Peninsula came to Medina to go with him. It is estimated that around 100,000 Muslims took part in this pilgrimage and went with the Prophet, who was already 63 years old.

The Prophet and his companions left Medina and made their way to Mecca. During the journey, Muhammad (saw) taught the pilgrims the rites and regulations of Hajj as they were conveyed to him by divine revelation from Allah (swt). The Hajj is based on practices that date to the Prophet Ibrâhîm (as) and his son Isma'il (as). Several verses in the Holy Quran deal with the various aspects of the great pilgrimage and its significance. For example, Sura 2:196-203 (Al-Baqara - The Cow) and Sura 22:27-30 (Al-Hajj - The Pilgrimage) deal with the duties and rituals of the pilgrimage.

Muhammad (saw) and thousands of Muslims entered Mecca in their Ihram attire and performed the Tawaf al-Qudum (welcoming Tawaf) by circling the Ka`ba seven times in a counterclockwise direction. They then performed the Sa'i, the walking back and forth between the hills of Safa and Marwa.

The departure for Mina a few days later marks the beginning of the actual Hajj rituals. The Prophet Muhammad (saw) and his companions set out from Mecca to Mina, roughly five kilometers from the city gates. This day is also known as "Yawm at-Tarwiyah" (day of watering/ water supply). Immediately after the morning prayer (Fajr), they set off for Mina. Upon arrival, they set up their tents and prepared for the upcoming rituals. The Muslims spent the day and night mainly in prayer. The Prophet and his companions used this time to prepare themselves spiritually for the most important day of the Hajj, the day of Arafat.

The next morning, Prophet Muhammad (saw) and his companions went to Arafat from Mina after praying. Arafat is a wide plain and lies about 20 kilometers east of Mecca. (See 5. on map 2) In the plain lies a small hill called Jabal al-Rahma (Mountain of Mercy), which has a special spiritual significance. This was where the Prophet Adam (as) and his wife Hawwa reunited after expulsion from paradise. The Masjid Namirah (Namirah Mosque) was later built on this site and is now an important pilgrimage site.

After they arrived in Arafat, Muhammad (saw) rested briefly and then prayed the noon (Dhuhr) and afternoon (Asr) prayers. The Prophet then climbed the hill Jabal al-Rahma (also known as Arafat Mountain) to deliver the sermon that later became known as the famous farewell sermon (Khutbat al-Wada) and has touched and guided millions of Muslims to this day. Muhammad (saw) reminded his followers of the central teachings and principles of Islam. He emphasized the equality of all human beings, regardless of race or ethnicity, and explained that all are descended from Adam (as) and Hawwa. He then explained to his captivated audience that the life, property, and honor of every Muslim are inviolable:

> "Verily! Your blood, your property, and your honor are sacred to each other (i.e., Muslims) like the sanctity of this day of yours, this month of yours, and this city of yours. It is incumbent upon those who are present to inform those who are absent, for those who are absent may understand (what I have said) better than the listeners who are present."
> Sahih al-Bukhari, Book 3, Hadith 67

He also called on men to treat their wives fairly. He reminded them of the importance of observing the five pillars of Islam: the profession of faith, prayer, fasting, the alms, and pilgrimage. The Prophet reiterated the strict prohibition of riba (usury), and reminded Muslims to always follow the laws and teachings of the Holy Quran and the Sunnah (the traditions, actions, and sayings of Muhammad (saw)):

> "I have left you two things to abide by so that you do not go astray as long as you follow them: The Book of Allah and the Sunnah of His Prophet."
> Al-Muwatta by Imam Malik, Book 46, Hadith 3

The Prophet and the pilgrims spent the rest of the day with the Wuquf (Standing before God / Dwelling Ceremony). Muhammad (saw) said the following dua (supplication), among others:

Arabic text:

لَا إِلَهَ إِلَّا ٱللَّهُ وَحْدَهُ لَا شَرِيكَ لَهُ، لَهُ ٱلْمُلْكُ وَلَهُ ٱلْحَمْدُ،
وَهُوَ عَلَىٰ كُلِّ شَيْءٍ قَدِيرٌ

Transliteration: "La ilaha illallah wahdahu la sharika lah,
lahul-mulku wa lahul-hamdu wa huwa 'ala kulli shay'in
qadeer."

Translation: "There is no god but Allah, the One and Only,
who has no partner. To Him belongs dominion and to Him
belongs praise, and He has power over all things."

Source: This supplication is considered one of the best
supplications for the Day of Arafat. Prophet Muhammad
(saw) said:

"The best supplication is the supplication on the day of
Arafat, and the best thing that I and the prophets before me
have said is: 'There is no god but Allah, the One and Only,
who has no partner. To Him belongs the dominion and to
Him belongs the praise, and He has power over all things."

Source: Muwatta Malik Book 20, Hadith 255, and Jami`
at-Tirmidhi 3585

The pilgrims remained on the plain until sunset, praying, listening to the Prophet's recitation of the Quran, and asking Allah (swt) for forgiveness.

After sunset, Muhammad (saw) and his followers set off for Muzdalifa. Upon arrival, the pilgrims looked for places in the open air to spend the night. Together with the Prophet, they performed the Maghrib prayer (evening prayer) and the Isha prayer (night prayer).

After saying their prayers, the pilgrims began to collect small pebbles they would need for the stoning ritual in Mina the next day. The pebbles should be about the size of a chickpea. The pilgrims then spent the night outdoors. This symbolized the simplicity and equality of all pilgrims before Allah (swt), regardless of their social or economic status.

The next morning, they prayed the Fajr prayer (morning prayer) before making their way back to Mina.

Once there, Muhammad (saw) threw seven pebbles onto the great pillar (Jamarat al-Aqaba) to symbolically stone the devil, saying "Allahu Akbar" (Allah is the greatest). The believers did the same as Muhammad (saw). The great pillar (Jamarat al-Aqaba) in Mina represents the place where the Prophet Ibrâhîm (as) resisted the temptation of the Shaitan (devil) by throwing stones at him. The Shaytaan had urged Ibrâhîm (as) to resist the command of Allah (swt). The ritual symbolizes resistance to evil and devotion to Allah (swt). There are also two other pillars in Mina: Jamarat al-Sughra (small pillar) and Jamarat al-Wusta (middle pillar). These also mark places where Ibrâhîm (as) resisted the temptations of shaitan, but they are only thrown with pebbles on the days of Tashriq.

After the symbolic stoning of the great pillar, Muhammad (saw) sacrificed several camels. The sacrifices marked the beginning of the Eid al-Adha festival. It commemorates the willingness of Ibrâhîm (as) to sacrifice his son

Isma'il (as) for Allah (swt). The meat of the sacrificed animals was divided into three parts: one part for the family, one part for friends and neighbors, and one part for the poor and needy.

After sacrificing the camels, the Prophet Muhammad (saw) shaved his hair - a symbol of purity and humility. Men shave the entire head or shorten the hair, while women only cut off a small strand.

The pilgrims then made their way to Mecca under the leadership of Muhammad (saw). There they performed the Tawaf al-Ifadah (main tawaf). This tawaf is a central ritual of the Hajj and, unlike the Tawaf al-Qudum (welcoming tawaf), is still obligatory for pilgrims today.

In the evening of the same day, the community around the Prophet set off again for Mina to spend the days of Tashriq there.

When they arrived there, the Prophet began the stoning ritual (Ramy al-Jamarat), in which he threw seven pebbles at each of the three pillars: Jamarat al-Sughra (small pillar), Jamarat al-Wusta (medium pillar) and Jamarat al-Aqaba (large pillar). Each throw was accompanied by the invocation "Allahu Akbar" (Allah is the greatest).

During the days of Tashriq, the Prophet and the pilgrims spent much of their time in prayer and remembrance of Allah (swt). They also sent supplications (Dua) to Allah (swt). After the obligatory prayers, they would recite the takbir: "Allahu Akbar, Allahu Akbar, la ilaha illallah, wallahu Akbar, Allahu Akbar, walillahil-hamd" (Allah is the greatest, Allah is the greatest, there is no god but Allah, and Allah is the greatest, Allah is the greatest, and all praise is due to Allah).

On the second day of Tashriq, Prophet Muhammad (saw) and his followers repeated the stoning ritual by throwing seven pebbles at each of the three pillars. After the ritual, the pilgrims could leave Mina and return to Mecca. This is known as "Nafar Awwal" ("the first group to leave"). The Prophet Muhammad (saw) allowed the pilgrims to return to Mecca if they wished, but he stayed in Mina until the next day.

On the last day of Tashriq, Muhammad (saw) and the pilgrims performed the stoning ritual one last time. They also performed daily prayers, recited duas, and honored Allah (swt). Then they returned to Mecca led by the Prophet.

When they arrived in the city, Muhammad (saw), accompanied by many other pilgrims, performed the Tawaf al-Wada (farewell tawaf). As before every tawaf, the wudu (ritual purification) was performed first, and then, starting from the black stone, the Ka`ba was circled seven times in a counterclockwise direction. This marked the end of the first, and last, Hajj of Muhammad (saw) and the Prophet returned to Medina.

Chapter

8

The Death of the Prophet Muhammad (saw)

Shortly after he arrived in Medina the Prophet suddenly fell ill. The illness began in May of the year 632. Muhammad (saw) suffered from fever and headaches and his condition worsened over time. Nevertheless, Muhammad (saw) still preached several times in the mosque despite his illness. Although he was in pain, he went to the mosque to lead his community. This is narrated in the following hadith:

"Abu Sa'id al-Khudri reported: The Prophet Muhammad (saw) came out when he was ill and sat on the pulpit. He said, 'Allah has given one of His servants a choice between what this world has to offer and what is with Allah, and he has chosen what is with Allah.
Sahih Muslim 2382a

When the Prophet became increasingly unwell, he asked Abu Bakr (ra) to lead the prayers for the congregation. In the last days of his life, Muhammad (saw) spent most of his time with his wife Aisha (ra).

Aisha (ra) reported: "The Prophet Muhammad (saw) said during his last illness: 'Prayer! The prayer! And what your right hand possesses."
Sunan Abi Dawud 5156

Muhammad (saw) thus emphasized the immense importance of prayer (salat) in the life of a Muslim. It was important to him that Muslims do not neglect prayer and perform it regularly and sincerely. The second part of his statement refers to the responsibility towards those who are under the care of a Muslim, including servants and slaves. The Prophet urged them to treat these people well, to grant them their rights, and to treat them justly and mercifully.

After the morning prayer on June 8, 632, Abu Bakr (ra) visited the Prophet. It seemed as if Muhammad's (saw) illness would subside. So, Muhammad's (saw) closest companion returned to his house. But during the day, the Prophet's health deteriorated considerably.

Shortly before his death, he murmured that he wanted Allah (swt) to admit him to the highest companions - the prophets of Islam who had died long ago. This is narrated in the following hadith:

> *Aisha (ra) reported: "I heard the Prophet (saw) say in his illness, from which he died, 'O Allah, forgive me and have mercy on me, and let me join the highest companions.' He repeated this several times, and I understood that he was choosing the Hereafter."*
> *Sahih al-Bukhari 5674*

Aisha (ra) also reported:

> *"I saw the Messenger of Allah (saw) dying, and there was a cup of water with him. He put his hand in the cup and wiped his face with the water, then he said, 'O Allah, help me through the agony and pain of death.*
> *Jami` at-Tirmidhi 978*

This special man, our Prophet Muhammad (saw), died on June 8, 632 in a room of his wife Aisha's house, which was directly next to the Prophet's Mosque. In Medina and far beyond, the Prophet's death caused great grief and consternation. Many companions of Muhammad (saw) initially refused to accept the death of their beloved Prophet. Among them was Umar ibn al-Khattab (ra) who threatened those who claimed that the Prophet had died.

When Abu Bakr (ra) received the news, he rode on his horse directly to the house of Aisha (ra), his daughter and the Prophet's widow. He entered and found the Prophet resting peacefully.

Aisha (ra) reported this in the following hadith:

"Then Abu Bakr came and unveiled the face of the Messenger of Allah ((ﷺ), kissed him, and said, "My father and mother be sacrificed to you, (O Messenger of Allah ((ﷺ)), you are beautiful in life and in death. By Allah, in Whose hands is my life, Allah will never let you taste death twice.""
Sahih al-Bukhari 3667, 3668

The expression, "My father and mother be sacrificed to you," is an idiom used to express deep affection and devotion. It meant that the person was willing to sacrifice everything, including the lives of his parents, for the beloved person. Saying this, Abu Bakr (ra) emphasized his appreciation and deep respect for the Prophet Muhammad (saw).

After his Faithful Companion confirmed the Prophet's death, he went to the mosque where the community was already gathered. Abu Bakr (ra) stepped forward and delivered his famous speech.

He said: "O people, whoever worships Muhammad, Muhammad is dead. But whoever worships Allah, Allah is alive and does not die."

Then he recited the verse from the Holy Quran, which is written in Sura 3:144 (Aal-Imran - the clan of Imran):

The wise words of Abu Bakr (ra) had a profound effect on the listeners. His speech helped them accept the reality of the beloved Prophet's death and focus on continuing their faith and duties towards Allah (swt). Moreover, the speech laid the foundation for the election of Abu Bakr (ra) as the first caliph and leader of the Muslims after the death of Muhammad (saw).

The Prophet's body was washed (ghusl) according to Islamic burial rituals. His closest relatives, Ali ibn Abi Talib (ra), Abbas ibn Abdul-Muttalib (ra), the Prophet's uncle, and his sons, Qutham and Fadl ibn Abbas, carried out the task. After ablution, the body was wrapped in three white cotton cloths that had neither seams nor decorations.

The Janaza prayer (funeral prayer) was then performed without an imam. Instead, the Muslims came in small groups to the room of Aisha (ra) to perform the prayer for their beloved Prophet. The men prayed first, followed by the women, and finally the children.

After the completion of the Janaza prayer, the body of Muhammad (saw) was prepared for burial. Then Muhammad (saw) was buried exactly where he had died - in the room of his wife Aisha (ra). The burial site was prepared directly under the deathbed. This was his express wish, as he once said that prophets should be buried in the place where they die. The former companions dug an L-shaped grave (lahd). They then gently laid the deceased prophet in the grave with his face facing the Qibla (Mecca). The closest relatives and companions - including Ali ibn Abi Talib (ra), Abbas ibn Abdul-Muttalib (ra) and his sons, as well as important companions such as Abu Bakr (ra) - threw earth on the grave and said supplications.

After the Prophet's burial, the Muslim community went through a period of deep mourning. The urgent question of leadership was answered by the election of Abu Bakr (ra) as the first caliph. Under his leadership, the unity and stability of the community was ensured, and important measures were taken for the defense and propagation of Islam. The collection of the Holy Quran and the preservation of the hadiths were crucial in preserving the legacy of Prophet Muhammad (saw) for us and generations to come.

Chapter
9

The Legacy of the Prophet Muhammad (saw): The Lord of Hearts

The Prophet Muhammad (saw), peace and blessings be upon him, was the light of humanity, the messenger of mercy and the herald of peace. His arrival marked the beginning of a new era, a beacon of truth and justice. He was the embodiment of mercy and the epitome of a noble character. His gentleness, wisdom, patience, and kindness are unmatched and at the same time everlasting. He was the most truthful and trustworthy, a man whose words and deeds were always in harmony. His love and compassion for the poor, orphans, and oppressed was boundless. He taught that true greatness lies in humility, strength in forgiveness, and power in gentleness.

Muhammad (saw) led the believers with infinite wisdom and tireless patience. In times of hardship and injustice, he was a steadfast institution of justice. He brought unity and brotherhood to a fragmented world, and his example of leadership was always just and merciful. In Medina, he founded the first Islamic community on the principles of tolerance, justice, and equality. He showed true leadership lies in service to the community and taught by his example the importance of compassion.

The Prophet enlightened people's hearts and led them from the darkness of ignorance into the light of knowledge towards Islam. His call to Allah (swt) as the only God broke the chains of polytheism and led humanity to its true destiny. He laid the foundations of civilization by defending the rights of women, children, and slaves, and integrated the principles of social justice and equality into society. His teachings and example laid the ethical and moral foundations that continue inspiring and guiding humanity today.

The Quran, which the Prophet Muhammad (saw) conveyed to mankind, is the timeless word of Allah (swt) and the most important part of his legacy. It was revealed to the Prophet over 23 years by the angel Jibril. Muhammad (saw) recited the verses revealed to him and many of his companions memorized them and wrote them on various materials such as palm leaves, parchment, and bones. After the Prophet's death, the Quran was compiled in a standardized written form. This was initially done under the leadership of the first caliph Abu Bakr (ra), who ensured that the various fragments and oral traditions were collected. Later, a final and standardized version of the Quran was created to avoid differences in recitation. This version was reproduced and sent to the most important Islamic centers to preserve the authenticity of the revelations of Allah (swt).

The legacy of Muhammad (saw) lives on in the hearts of billions of believers who spread peace and righteousness in his name. His life is an eternal guide for all those who strive for truth, justice, and mercy. His Sunnah is a gift and an inexhaustible source of wisdom and is still today an ideal example of how to lead a fulfilled and righteous life. His influence on history and civilization is profound and everlasting. The name of Muhammad (saw) will forever evoke reverence and love in the hearts of believers.

Muhammad (saw) is the seal of the prophets, the perfect light of the divine guidance of Allah (swt), and the bringer of peace. His achievements are unsurpassed, his character is unmatched, and his legacy will shine eternally. May Allah (swt) bless and elevate him to the highest levels of Paradise, where he shall dwell in peace and honor forever. He is the beloved Prophet, teacher, and leader. Thanks be to Allah (swt) for His immeasurable mercy in sending us Muhammad (saw) as a role model.

Peace and blessings be upon the Prophet, today and forever.

Glossary

Adhan: Call to prayer.

Ahzab: Group/Confederation.

Ansar: Muslim helpers/supporters from Medina who took in the Muslims from Mecca in the city.

Aws: One of the most powerful tribes in Medina (before the Prophet's entry).

Barakah: The blessing (general, not just for a business).

Bay'at al-Ridwan: The oath of allegiance under the tree that the Muslims swore to Muhammad (saw) in Hudaybiyya.

Diya: The compensation payment/blood money.

Fajr prayer: Morning Prayer.

Ghanimah: Spoils of war.

Hajj: The great pilgrimage.

Hijrah: Emigration of the Prophet and his followers from Mecca to Medina.

Ihram: The pilgrim's robe.

Isha prayer: Night Prayer.

Isra and Mi'raj: The Prophet's Night Journey and Journey to Heaven.

Janaza prayer: Prayer for the dead.

Khazraj: One of the most powerful tribes in Medina (before the Prophet's entry).

Khutbat al-Wada: Farewell sermon of the Prophet.

Maghrib prayer: Evening Prayer.

Munafiqun: Religious hypocrite.

Muhajirun: Muslim emigrants from Mecca.

Nisab: Minimum assets for calculating zakat.

Qibla: Official direction of prayer towards Mecca.

Qisas: Principle of retribution according to Sharia law.

Rak'ah: The prayer unit.

Riba: Interest collection.

Sahaba: Companions of the Prophet.

Shahada: the profession of faith in Islam.

Sharia: The totality of Islamic laws and ethical standards.

Shura: Consulting.

Sunnah: Practice or behavior established by the Prophet.

Tala'a al-Badru 'Alayna: Song sung at the Prophet's entry into Medina.

Takbir: Shouting "Allahu Akbar," which means "Allah is the greatest."

Tawaf: circling the Ka`ba seven times clockwise.

Tawaf al-Ifadah: Main Tawaf.

Tawaf al-Qudum: Welcome Tawaf.

Tawaf al-Wada: Farewell Tawaf.

Ummah: the totality of all Muslims.

Wuquf: Standing before God (dwelling ceremony during the pilgrimage).

Yathrib: Original name of the city of Medina.

Yawm at-Tarwiyah: Day of watering/water supply.

Zakat: Compulsory tax for wealthy Muslims to benefit the needy.

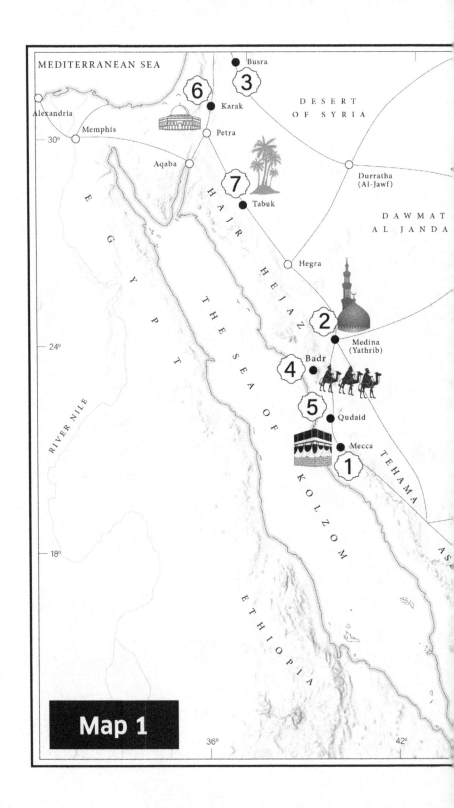

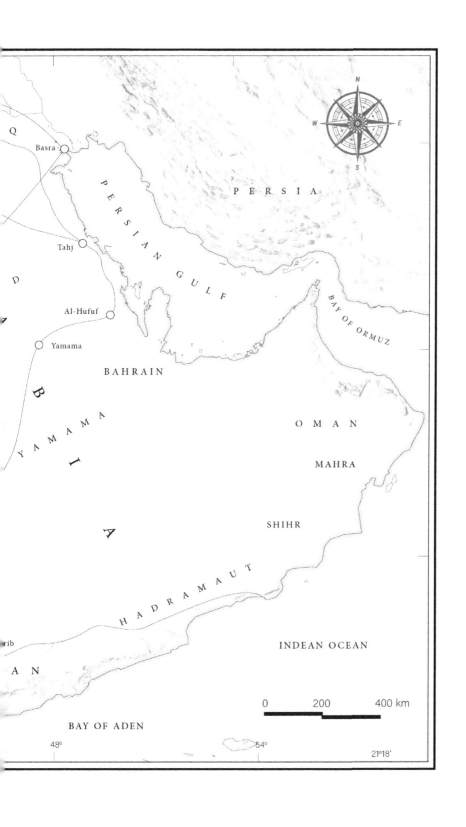

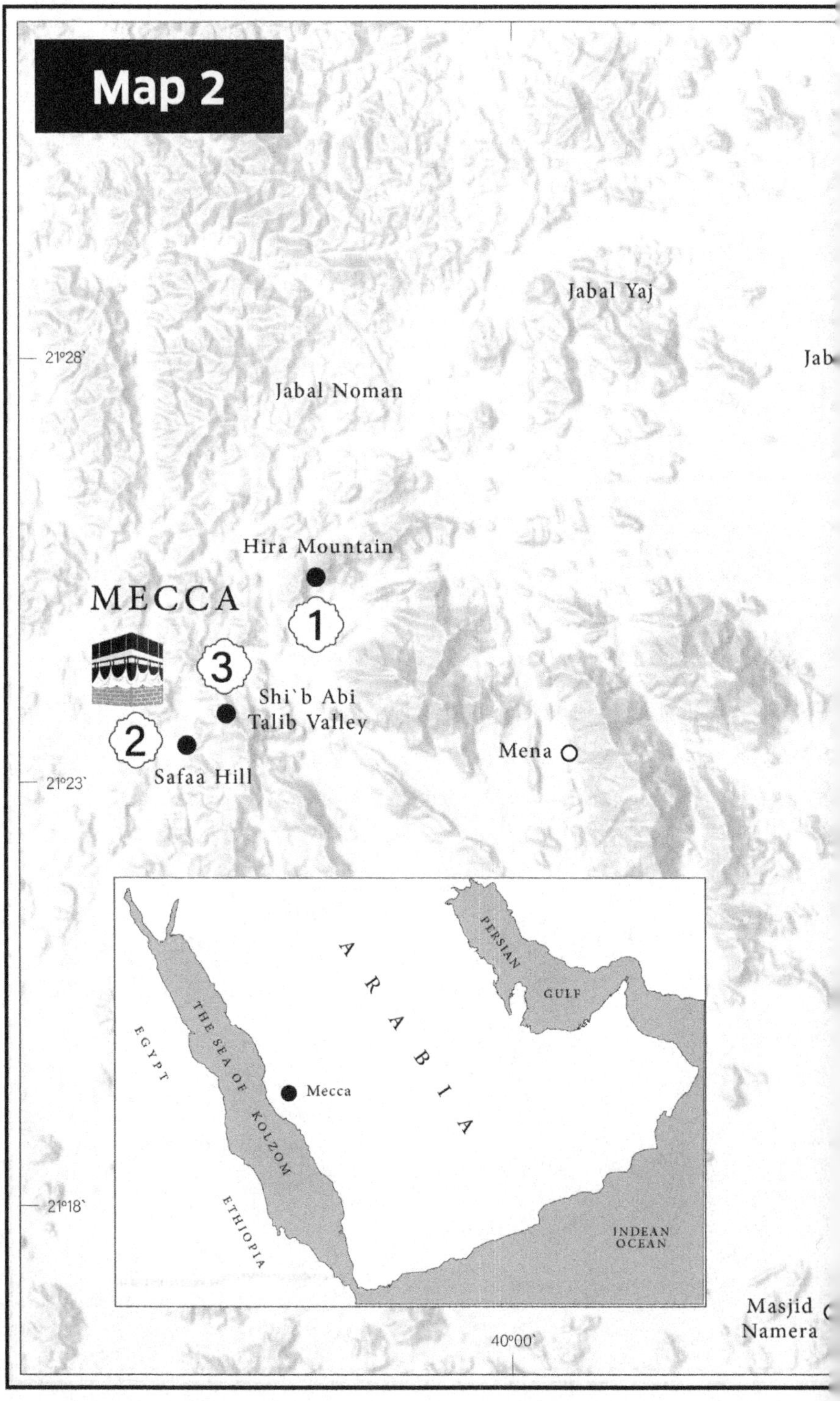

Map 2

Jabal Yaj

Jab

21°28'

Jabal Noman

Hira Mountain

MECCA

1

3

Shi`b Abi
Talib Valley

Mena ○

2

Safaa Hill

21°23'

A R A B I A

PERSIAN

GULF

EGYPT

THE SEA OF KOIZOM

Mecca

ETHIOPIA

INDEAN
OCEAN

21°18'

Masjid
Namera

40°00'

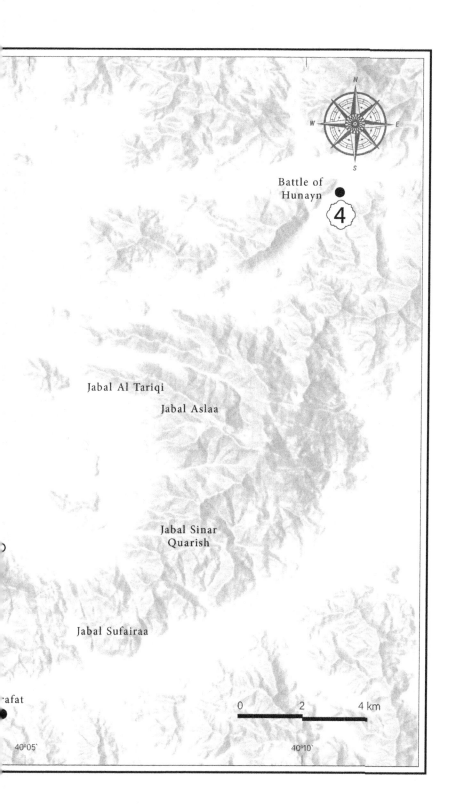

Battle of
Hunayn

④

Jabal Al Tariqi

Jabal Aslaa

Jabal Sinar
Quarish

Jabal Sufairaa

afat

0   2   4 km

40°05`                    40°10`

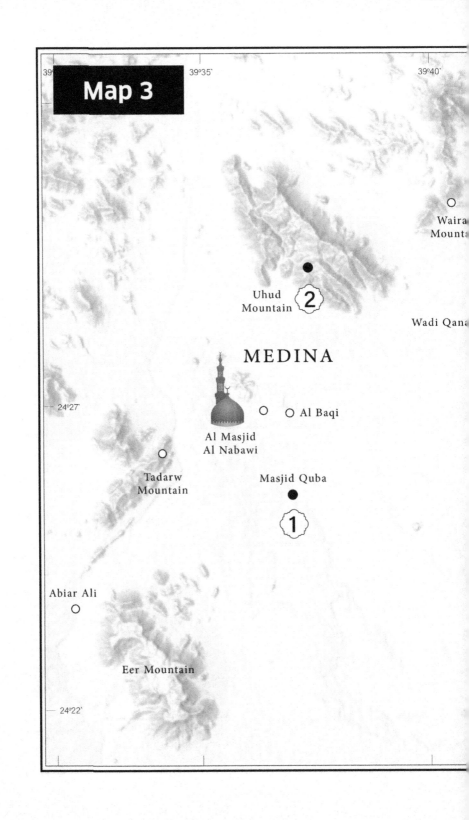

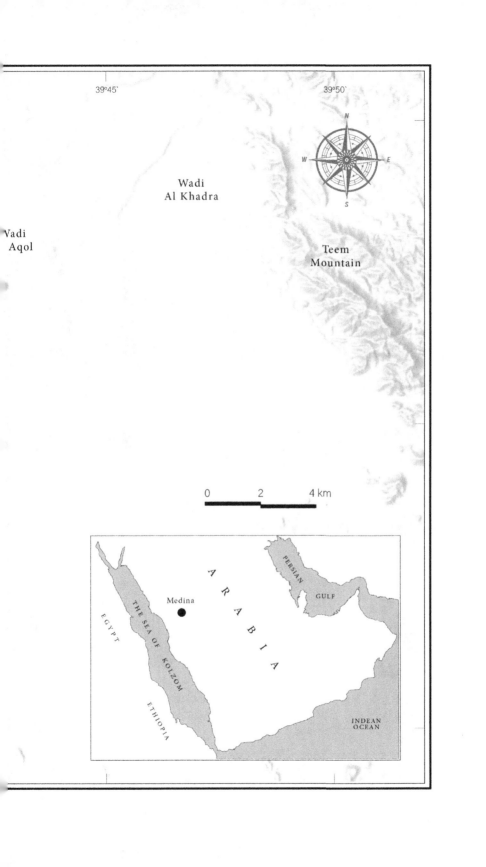

39°45`    39°50`

N
W   E
S

Wadi
Al Khadra

Wadi
Aqol

Teem
Mountain

0   2   4 km

A R A B I A

PERSIAN
GULF

Medina

EGYPT

THE SEA OF KOLZOM

ETHIOPIA

INDEAN
OCEAN

More books by

Islam Way

· · · · · · · · · · · · · · · · ·

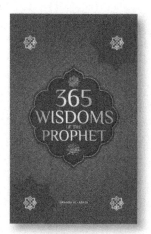

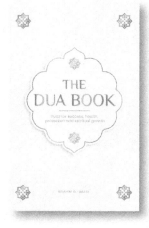

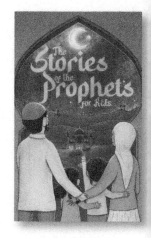

Islam Way is a collective of Arabic speakers, writers and translators who have set out to strengthen Islam in the world and reach as many people as possible with their life-enriching messages.

The team is made up of Muslims firmly rooted in their faith and eager to do their bit to strengthen Islam. The Prophet (ﷺ) said: 'Whoever motivates someone to do a good deed will receive the same reward as him' and this is the guiding principle of Islam Way.

Made in the USA
Las Vegas, NV
09 March 2025

19287477R00085